BEYOND THE BELL

'A "cause" is founded by an individual and the individual carries the "cause". A time comes when the "cause" starts carrying the individual. I think that is what is happening here—the "cause" called NSN has started carrying all of us. Let us continue to be worthy instruments to this noble cause of NSN and play our part in putting India at the top and building a better world in the process. Love how NSN is more than a school. It is a culture. What a time to be alive!'

—**mahātria Rā**
Spiritualist, Thought Leader and Diviner of infinitheism

'A school is built not by brick and mortar but by the thoughts, ideas, values and culture of the people in the school. My visit to NSN and interaction with the faculty was an opportunity to note that the school has leadership that ushers in a positive and growth mindset among all its stakeholders. The curricular engagement in the school offers a spiritual flavour to the learners, teaching them to be conscious and contributive rather than just pursuing success with a certification. I congratulate Chitra Prasad for comprehending this conceptual design and articulating it into a thought architecture in this book. *Beyond the Bell* would certainly help all educators to position their schools with a blend of spirituality and pragmatism. In a world that is becoming increasingly consumerist, the time is ripe for school leaders to reflect on the issues that challenge the next generation of learners. Facilitating learners to understand constructive collaboration between the individual and universal consciousness must become the foundation for a good schooling process. I am confident that this book will help educators to understand this significant objective.'

—**Dr G. Balasubramanian**
Former Director (Academics),
Central Board of Secondary Education (CBSE), Delhi;
Leader and Creative Head,
T-360: Learning Spaces, Bengaluru

'One can sense quite easily from the writings and persona of Chitra Prasad that she is the epitome of an empathetic soul. The laudable work that NSN Schools have been undertaking for society has left an almost unparalleled mark. Through this book, she will further inspire legions of educationists to emulate her journey through empathy and understanding of the true requirements of education at the ground level.'

—**Vivek Atray**
Ex-IAS; Motivational TEDx Speaker;
Author of *Finding Success Within*

'NSN made me a good human being, besides the strong academic footing that it gave me. I shall remain grateful till my last breath for this service. I wish this institution showers its choicest blessings to more students in the decades to come. Mangalani Bhavantu! I am sure this book is going to ignite young minds, and is going to be like a "Guru" for the educationists.'

—**Dushyanth Sridhar**
Vedic Speaker, Author, Director on Ancient Hindu Scriptures and an ex-NSNite

BEYOND THE BELL

Preparing Students for Life

CHITRA PRASAD

Published by
Rupa Publications India Pvt. Ltd 2025
7/16, Ansari Road, Daryaganj
New Delhi 110002

Sales centres:
Bengaluru Chennai Hyderabad
Jaipur Kathmandu Kolkata
Mumbai Prayagraj

Copyright © Chitra Prasad 2025
Photographs courtesy: Chitra Prasad

Copyright of the photographs vests with the respective photographer/copyright owner.

While every effort has been made to trace copyright holders and obtain permission, this has not been possible in all cases; any omissions brought to our attention will be remedied in future editions.

The views and opinions expressed in this book are the author's own and the facts are as reported by her, which have been verified to the extent possible, and the publishers are not in any way liable for the same.

All rights reserved.
No part of this publication may be reproduced, transmitted or stored in a retrieval system, in any form or by any means, electronic, mechanical, photocopying, recording or otherwise, without the prior permission of the publisher.

P-ISBN: 978-93-6156-412-3
E-ISBN: 978-93-6156-396-6

First impression 2025

10 9 8 7 6 5 4 3 2 1

The moral right of the author has been asserted.

Printed in India

This book is sold subject to the condition that it shall not, by way of trade or otherwise, be lent, resold, hired out or otherwise circulated, without the publisher's prior consent, in any form of binding or cover other than that in which it is published.

To my mother,
who embodied resilience and faith.
She bore the pain life inflicted on her like a warrior
and lived her life unruffled and unperturbed,
dedicating herself completely to the cause called NSN.
Today, the NSN Group of Schools stand as a testimony
to the indomitable spirit of this Iron Lady,
who would not be cowed down by fate.
Her life has left a lasting impression on my mind.

Contents

Foreword	*ix*
Author's Note	*xiii*
NSN School Song	*xvii*
And the Cause Chose Me	2
A Day at NSN	4
A Nation Builder	6
Teaching Is My Calling	9
School Is a Golden Triangle	11
Champions of Change	15
Lifting Society Through Education	17
Creating a Better World	20
Dare to be Different	22
Be a Pathbreaker	26
Why a Teacher has to be a Role Model	28
The Being and Becoming of a Teacher	31
The Demands of Your Role	33
Walk the Extra Mile	36
Empowering Mentors	39
Teacher Empowerment	43
An Overhaul	46
Aligning the Mind, Body and Soul	49
Leading the Changemakers	52
The Change Agents	56
A Worthy Life	58
Grow in Your Own Eyes	61
Post-pandemic Blues	62

Overcoming Challenges	65
Building Relationships	68
To Love and to be Loved	72
Work–Life Balance	74
Tightrope Walk	78
Anger Management	81
Volcanic Eruptions	84
Beyond the Comfort Zone	87
Get…Set…Go!	91
Dented Self-image	94
Body Shaming	98
Changing a Child's Perception	102
I am Unique	105
Fitness and Beyond	108
Staying Fit	111
Bouquet of Thanks	114
On-time All the Time	117
On-time, Every Time	120
Responsible Citizenship	123
Make Your Life Count	126
Attitude of Gratitude	129
A Grateful Heart	133
Spirituality in Education	135
Spiritual Alignment	138
One Best Practice of NSN	141
Mata, Pita, Guru, Deivam	144
The Creators of My Life	147

Foreword

I have known Chitra Prasad in four different capacities and would like to begin this foreword by sharing my experience of this towering personality in these four roles.

As a fellow seeker: That is how my relationship with Chitra first began. We both follow the spiritual path of infinitheism, divined by our beloved guru, mahātria. Within our fraternity of infinitheists, she is greatly admired as a person who is living a life of holistic abundance. While heading a huge brand like the NSN Group of Schools in Chennai, she continues to focus on her health, relationships and spiritual journey as a regular meditator for over a decade. All of us who know her get inspired by her as a multi-role wonder and actually wonder, how she does it all!

As a fellow educator: NSN has been following the Wonders of Words' (WoW) 3L (language + life + leadership skills) curriculum founded by me for seven years now. In these seven years of professional association, two things have impacted me tremendously. The first: Chitra's passion for bringing the best in the world to her students—how she gets personally involved with the growth of each of the 5,800 plus students (soon to be 7,000!) and how much she cares about her teachers and staff. Second: how prompt and proactive NSN has always been with completing investments and sending orders and reviews. Though these things seem insignificant, they go a long way in harbouring trust in anyone connected with NSN.

As a part of *The Breakthrough* book: In 2020, I wrote a book called *The Breakthrough*, published by Rupa, where I interviewed several individuals across the country and finally chose 11 of them to be featured for their incredible stories. Chitra's story of how she lost her father at the tender age of nine months, and how her widowed mother started NSN as a school in one room in the memory of her late husband touched me to the core. The nuances, the twists and turns, and the sheer grit and guts with which the mother–daughter have faced life and made NSN into what it is stands as testimony to the human spirit and its limitless power and possibilities.

As a student: When Chitra and I decided to come up with this book to aid fellow educators and create a community of like-minded (moreover, right-minded) people, we worked together for weeks on end so that this fine educator could pen her thoughts and ideas. I wondered how this blazing personality, with close to a two-decade age difference between us, would be as a student. Truth be told, I was a little nervous. I was happily and pleasantly surprised to see this legendary woman transform into a curious, humble and open-minded student, willing to learn and grow even in this area of playing with words. It was truly humbling and showed me how I should always keep the student within me alive, no matter what pinnacle of success I achieve. In fact, she made me realize that the best educators are those who keep the student within them alive and burning, and keep learning (and unlearning) to bring the best for their students.

Beyond the Bell is not just a book. It is a living testimonial of how much is possible for an educator to achieve with youngsters to get them ready for 'Life'. It is proof of the several decades of commitment that a leader has towards her students, teachers and even parents to make them their best versions. *Every word in this book is not written, it is lived, and hence, it will go straight to your heart.*

I truly wish we grow into a community of educators who come together for the well-being of every student in the country (to begin with) and take over the world at large. It is imperative to gift a beautiful future to the world.

Together, we are a miracle!

I have experienced this with Chitra, and I wish you experientially realize this as you read this book, connect with her and find ways to bring some of the best practices of NSN to your school or simply share your ideas and dreams with her and find ways to come together to empower hundreds and thousands of youths to live life as their best versions.

There must be a reason all of us have been chosen by Life for this noble profession. Let's make the most of it.

With my best wishes,
Megha Bajaj
Bestselling Author, Author–Mentor,
TEDx Speaker, Educator and Seeker
www.meghabajajwow.com

Author's Note

'Unintended consequences produce far greater results than intended consequences.'

—mahātria Rā

This is true of my life. As a reluctant educationist for whom educating students has become second nature and not just a passion, I dread to think of how I began my journey in this field with neither any formal training nor experience, so to speak. 'Where there is passion, competence can be developed,' says mahātria Rā. Becoming an educationist was a huge responsibility. There were innumerable challenges that needed to be handled. Quitting was the foremost thought in my mind because it had started to feel like a noose around my neck. To run an educational institution, one has to be a good leader; have skills in efficient human resource management, interpersonal communication, management, administration, finance, planning, curriculum designing and mentoring; be emotionally equanimous; and juggle various roles. It is indeed a tightrope to walk. All of this has to be done with grace and dignity.

Where was I supposed to begin? I focused all my energies on being an architect of NSN's future. Here I am, after almost three decades, beaming with pride at creating NSN the way it is today, celebrating my life as an educationist and loving every moment in school with vigour and as much enthusiasm as I had when I first began.

My mother created the NSN legacy after she had a tryst with destiny and was widowed at a very young age. She started

NSN Children's in 1968 to perpetuate the memory of my dad, Sri N.S.N. Menon. She became the reason for the unfolding of my innate potential. I owe her my heartfelt gratitude for being instrumental in revealing my life's purpose.

The school's strength is undoubtedly the principal, vice-principal, teaching faculty and all the other school staff, many of whom may be considered torchbearers and change agents. The school is continuously improving and growing only because of their sincere efforts, competence and contribution. The credit for the standards NSN has achieved and for the culture and ethos that prevail goes to them.

Furthermore, the trust reposed in us by the parents of our students and their support, goodwill and cooperation are propelling NSN to greater heights.

My heart beats for my students and is filled with love for them. They have given new meaning to my life and made me feel complete. They are the reason I look forward to going to school every morning; there is little I will not do for them. My students are the purpose of my life.

Megha Bajaj, a national bestselling author who has been associated with NSN for several years, came up with the idea of writing a book to share NSN's best practices. Every time she came to NSN, she experienced its energy. Through our interactions, she understood the philosophy that drives education at NSN; we focus on not only a child's becoming but also their being. This was unique to NSN. She believed that we could touch many more lives by sharing this philosophy with as many educationists as possible. This book took shape through her guidance and mentoring.

My various struggles in the profession, innumerable challenges from within and from the world outside and everyday stress were all magically replaced by breakthroughs in my profession, competence and confidence. My initiation into spirituality and my deep surrender to and faith in my spiritual guru, mahātria Rā, filled my life with positive vibes and energy. I began attracting holistic abundance into my life. Peace and harmony descended. I experienced a rebirth in every sense. My life transformed, and I began going with the flow.

NSN follows infinitheism, and the environment we provide our students and most of our best practices discussed in this book have been derived from its teachings and wisdom. Infinitheism refers to a path divined by mahātria Rā, which awakens humanity and encourages them to be on the path of holistic abundance. The beauty is that the leader's transformation aids in the transformation of all who are associated with the organization. NSN has integrated spirituality with education, which makes the institution unique in its practices as it takes us back to our roots.

Last but not the least, everything that has beautifully manifested in my life is because of the unconditional support of my family, that has given me the strength to face the challenges that came my way, and most importantly, the peace that prevails in my life, which helps me to focus on what I am passionate about with undivided attention.

I am sure this book will add value to the many ideas and practices you already follow in your school. It will certainly help you change the outlook of teachers and students and, most importantly, transform the school environment, which contributes to students' holistic growth. Let us all join hands, exchange ideas and take time to reflect so that we not only make schooling a great experience but also aid in the building of this great country by nurturing students for the nation.

NSN School Song

This song describes the best practices of NSN.

We are NSNites, we are NSNites, we are NSNites
We come from a school
That prepares us for life
Our learning goes beyond the classroom
Experiences that make us rich
Not only in knowledge and skills
But in our values too

We are NSNites, we are NSNites, we are NSNites
We come from a school
That helps us to look beyond
Me, mine and myself
To be of use to society
Developing a helping mentality
To serve with joy and vitality

We are NSNites, we are NSNites, we are NSNites
We come from a school
That deepens our gratitude
Towards our parents
Our teachers and all
Love and gratitude always fill our heart
We are taught this from the start

We are NSNites, we are NSNites, we are NSNites
We come from a school

That teaches us to live
With dignity, pride and grace
We value commitment, equality and excellence
We will strive to be the best
In what we choose to do

We are NSNites, we are NSNites, we are NSNites
We will practice *ahimsa*
We will make our life count
We will make our country proud
We will live to look up to ourselves
We will make it big in life
We are the future, we are the future
We are from NSN

Feel blessed to be amidst children

And the Cause Chose Me

HE sends you to Earth
Raw and unprepared
Whispering a PURPOSE
In your ear.
But earthly life
Takes over
From here,
And the mortal journey begins…

In the din of life,
The hustle and bustle
And the sights you behold,
The whisper is forgotten.
As emotions take hold
And you live
In a world of pain and pleasure,
Forgetting the whisper,

Then comes a game-changer in life
Of choosing to be a leader.
Oh! how I dreaded
To be an educator.
My smile froze!!!
Yet courageously I ventured
Into the unknown
Feeling sad and forlorn.

Time flitted…
Unbounded joy
And happiness engulfed.
I was no more
The reluctant educationist I was.
Every moment,
Every heartbeat
Took me closer to HIM…

Every day became my Valentine's Day,
And I rejoiced
In the love
Of the little angels
Who became
The PURPOSE of my life.
And, in a moment,
The whisper was loud and clear.

With overwhelming gratitude,
I looked up towards HIM
In prayerfulness.
Tears trickling
Whispering…
'Thank you, God, for choosing me
As Thy instrument
I am truly, truly, blessed!'

A Day at NSN

I wake up to a new morning
With a wave of gratitude in my heart
For filling my being
With a sense of responsibility
And overwhelming love.

I enter the school with a smile,
Waving out to those little angels,
Already arrived and ready to start,
Screaming out to me 'Happy morning'
With so much life and vigour.

Straight to the temple I go,
Whispering a prayer to my Lord,
To hold my children in His embrace.
Touching the floor, feeling blessed, as I step in,
Knowing that I am His Instrument.

Overlooking every action of mine,
In my sacred space, are the guardian angels of my life
Whose grace, blessings and presence
I always carry in my heart,
Without whom I am nothing.

The oath we take every day,
Reiterates to the teachers
The role they play,

The sacredness of who we ought to be
To nurture the students with motherly care.

Silence descends and peace prevails
As the school goes into non-doing.
'Life is Beautiful' wafting in the air.
The oath of originality and the self-affirmation that follows
Are moments to reckon within a child's life.

The most defining morning time
Prepares them for the life ahead,
Not forgetting the knowledge imparted.
Classrooms bustling with high energy.
Eyes asking for most and more.

Social, moral, spiritual, intellectual growth
And much more is experienced in a day.
A holistic education is the best way.
A school with a difference
That takes education beyond
The realm of one's perception
Of what a school ought to be.

A Nation Builder

'One teacher, one book, one pen can change the world.'

—Malala Yousafzai

The Annual Performance Review meeting was happening at the NSN Group of Schools. Every department was presenting the statistics of students' performance in their subject, their plan, how much of it they achieved, what worked, what did not work, etc. I could notice their commitment, sincerity and pride when they spoke about their achievements and breakthrough moments, how a slow learner became a topper in the board exam, students' capabilities, and more. Although not all were impressive, some of them were overwhelming. In fact, one particular department's achievement was so motivating that we got them to present it to the other teachers in both schools (NSN Chromepet and NSN Memorial).

'It's never crowded along the extra mile.'

—Wayne Dyer

When we commit ourselves to our profession and sincerely do our work, we become a benchmark to the rest. Such people always stretch themselves and go beyond the call of duty. They are passionate about their profession. Doing work that energizes you rather than tires you is your *swadharma*. At NSN, we call our teachers mentors as they are expected to mould their students and not just impart knowledge. When a teacher is referred to as a mentor, their approach towards their profession shifts. They will look at their responsibility towards students differently.

At NSN, a mentor's day begins with Dr A.P.J. Abdul Kalam's 11-point oath. It makes them realize their vital role in nation-building through moral leadership. The oath is read every day to reiterate who they are and what their responsibilities are. Sincerely reading the oath will deeply influence the subconscious and enable the teacher to grow in the right direction. However, this has to be our endeavour. It is like a self-affirmation. Saying it every day will help us become model teachers. Everyone in the teaching profession must have a copy of this 11-point oath. Though he only taught college students, Dr Kalam thought like a school teacher. He had the right attributes, which were much more than what we can know from the oath. He was a spiritualist and was absolutely immersed in his profession, which he saw as a calling.

A teacher has to continuously build capacities in teaching and equip themself by imbibing the right qualities. Hence, the timeless wisdom of infinitheism—a path that inspires us to achieve breakthroughs—is shared with them every day to fill their minds with great thoughts so they can spread nobility in thought and action among students. Continuous professional development is also provided to enhance their skills and subject knowledge. Calling myself a nation builder broadens my perspective about my role as an educationist. Each one of us should know that our actions and inactions impact the nation. We are, in fact, shaping the nation's destiny. Roll up your sleeves to take up the challenging profession of a teacher, a creator. Lift your collars up if you are already a nation-builder.

Teaching is the mother of all professions. Every professional has to go through the hands of a teacher. Nobody can bypass them. The teacher is a kingmaker. They have the power to transform the world. A nation can be uplifted only through education and employment. A teacher has to walk the talk as children learn more from what they see than from what they hear. So a teacher needs to behave in such a way that their life becomes a message for students, which is a tall order indeed. This is the expectation in a country that has rich traditions and culture. We need to reflect on our thoughts and actions. You are His chosen one if you are a teacher. Not everyone can become a teacher.

Teaching Is My Calling

Eager and excited they come
To experience
Something new every day.
I plan meticulously,
Up to the last detail,
Missing out nothing
To keep them engrossed.
Knowledge keeps evolving.
I keep exploring
New ways to reach,
For I am a teacher.

A potpourri of talents,
With attitudes galore.
They are a handful,
Outsmarting the rest
All the time.
Some innocent, some guile.
I embark every day
On a new journey,
Relentless,
Alert, with loving firmness,
For I am a mentor.

Worming my way
Into their hearts,
Taking them in my hands,
Making them accountable,

And responsible citizens too.
Moulding them,
Chiselling them,
Sculpting them
To discover
Their best version,
For I am a nation builder too.

Love is the ingredient
That creates a bond.
Modelling is the way
I lead them forward.
Commitment is what
Helps me stay focused.
Rooted in my values,
Passion is my driving force.
I know,
I create, I evolve, I maximize.
My work is my prayer unto Him.

School Is a Golden Triangle

'There are two things children should get from their parents: roots and wings.'

—Johann Wolfgang von Goethe

Whenever we educationists meet at a conclave, we have so much to talk about—apprise and update each other on the latest developments, enquire about each other's well-being, and share and discuss our challenges. We speak the same language, so we have much in common. It is also time for us to catch up with other educators, which is not possible otherwise because we are all caught up with our work in school. I found one pain point common amongst all of them, which, I guess, some of you are also going through: parents' unnecessary interference in school matters. Parents are also grumbling a lot in WhatsApp groups.

All school heads are putting in so much effort to provide quality education to students. Teachers are playing their part by sparing no effort in imparting knowledge to students and moulding them into responsible individuals. We understand that parents are toiling hard at their workplace to educate their children in a good school. Students are also trying their best to achieve high scores. Nevertheless, why is there a strained relationship between parents and the school and between students and teachers?

'Education is a shared commitment between dedicated teachers, motivated students and enthusiastic parents with high expectations.'

—Bob Beauprez

A school is a golden triangle. The teacher, student and parent should have a smooth and amicable relationship. The teacher and parent significantly influence the student. It is a huge challenge to deal with parents' emotions. Social media have become a platform where people just vent their emotions and frustrations. There is a lot of disturbance in people's minds. Work pressure, children not being focused, strained relationships, differences of opinion between parents and discord in the family and financial issues could be some reasons why parents throw tantrums. I would call these misplaced emotions.

Many adults suffer from this and create emotional drama wherever they go. School is not the only place. There is no respect for the head of the institution or the teacher either in non-verbal or verbal communication. Am I right? Words are just let loose. They don't realize that their child is a witness to this drama. I have had instances when children have apologized for their parents' misbehaviour. The environment provided in school is such that students are quite aware of what is right and wrong. The prevailing culture is one of respect. Children who grow up in such an environment are clear about the value system.

I believe that parents should do their due diligence before admitting their wards to a school. Once they admit them, they should go with the flow. They should not question the grammar of the place but trust the school. That would be a perfect marriage between parents and the school. Threatening each other in a marriage also leads to an unsavoury relationship. This is true of a school, too. Threatening the school to abide by their demands and calling the media to complain about their child's school but continuing their education in the same school demonstrates a lack of clarity in what they really want.

Now, who should teach parents about appropriate behaviour? At NSN, we have a Reach Out Programme at the beginning of the academic year for all levels. We tell parents what they can expect from the school and what the school expects from them. The system is transparent. We have also created a parent feedback e-mail ID. The e-mails sent are read by the correspondent, who is the administrative head of the institution and only responds to queries regarding management policies. Everything else is forwarded to the principal. A copy of the principal's reply to the parent is sent by the principal to the correspondent as well.

When parents make unreasonable demands, the principal calls them in person and explains the situation. Even those who are not convinced by our e-mail reply are responded to in person and a satisfactory report is taken from them. This is how feedback and complaints are handled. Each parent may have suggestions, but we cannot run a school based on a thousand opinions. So we categorically tell Parent–Teacher Association (PTA) members what we can and cannot implement. While suggestions are welcome, they can be implemented only if they are feasible.

'Every home is a university and the parents are the teachers.'

—Mahatma Gandhi

Misbehaviour at the school gate occurs occasionally. Allegations are made against the school if it insists on punctuality. The physical education teacher is insulted and spoken to disrespectfully for insisting on school rules. We call the parents and speak to them so that they realize their mistake. Parents do not realize that they are poisoning the minds of their wards against the school and teachers. The parents' behaviour calls for a lot of patience and an understanding of human psychology. Getting one's ego involved with parents only makes matters worse. At NSN, we focus more on how we can influence the behaviour of students, rather than be concerned about the impact of parents' influence on children's behaviour. We are trying hard to ensure a child's holistic development, which requires the right environment at home as well.

I would like to know how each of you deals with the parents' immature behaviour. The emotional drama will not help either of us. In fact, it will only lead to a showdown. Instead of reacting, it helps when we respond to the situation. When the head of the institution responds calmly, it diffuses the situation. When we are able to positively influence the students, they, in turn, will influence their parents. So we can keep working continuously with the children. I am sure they are convinced about the school's good intentions. All we can do is give students a comfortable experience in school. We can establish a strong relationship with them. Then, dealing with such parents will be a lot easier. Every adverse situation only makes us stronger and better. The world then paves the way for a resolute soul.

Champions of Change

They enter the gates
With a glint of hope
Of a day
That promises
A comfortable stay
All day.

The words we speak,
The way we treat,
The comfort we give,
The hands we hold,
Are the souls
We soothe.

Heaven or hell,
They should tell.
Foster a climate
Of love and trust.
Freedom of expression
Is what they seek.

School or home,
The environment
Plays a pivotal role.
Be the Guardian Angel
They can connect
With their heart.

The positive vibes
They receive from you
Can give their life
An upward look.
Life will be bright
Only if you are right.

Judge them not
For they are frail.
Teach them how to be.
They will learn.
In the years to come,
Prim and proper they will be.

Attach no rewards
To what is right.
They will learn
To earn a name.
Morals and ethics
Will be the way

Foster them with love.
Guide them all the way.
Never label them.
They are the future.
Remember to nurture them,
Oh, champions of change!

Lifting Society Through Education

'Education is the most powerful weapon which you can use to change the world.'

—Nelson Mandela

I received a call from the school bus driver's daughter, asking if she could meet me. I gave her a time convenient to me. I knew that she had good news to share, probably about some promotion in her office. She studied at NSN, and her higher education in engineering was sponsored by us. She came home, and we exchanged pleasantries. Soon after, she settled down and joyfully told me that she had been working at a leading software company for one year. Now, they had offered her a site project in Spain. She would be leaving soon. Her husband and son would join her in a few months. My joy knew no bounds to hear the good news because I knew her background and how she had proved to the world that with a good education, one can make it big in life.

This is also the story of a boy who went on to become an engineer in the mining industry; his father was also our school bus driver. So many of our support staff's children are doing their undergraduate studies, and we sponsor their higher education, too, apart from providing them free education in school. These children have absolutely no support for academics from their parents or for their future plans. Their sheer willpower and drive enabled them to excel. Witnessing their self-confidence grow is a pleasant experience, and sponsoring their education is a joy. Their families have been financially uplifted to a different level.

At least 30 per cent of our students are first-generation learners. The school gives fee concessions and exemptions to meritorious students from underprivileged families. Some of these students get such high marks that one cannot ignore or overlook them. As many as 450 students get free education every year from NSN. A sum of more than INR 1,00,00,000 is set aside for their education. Their higher education is also taken care of.

Only through education and employment can we uplift the nation. In a school, we do both. So many families can be lifted out of poverty if they can be educated or employed. 'Give a man a fish and you feed him for a day. Teach a man to fish and you feed him for a lifetime.' Being able to give calls for a generous heart. Giving is an attitude. We can create a revolution in the country if each of us decides to uplift the masses. We can change the destiny of thousands of families and that of the nation. Intelligence is rampant amongst the underprivileged; all they need is a breakthrough. Money should never be an obstacle for them. If a percentage of the surplus every educational institution has can be directed towards uplifting the masses by providing education, it would be a very thoughtful gesture.

As an educator, I have found that first-generation learners are raring to go. They just need an opening. Believe me, the way some of them excel will stun you. The high marks some of them score, the confidence with which they make presentations in the general assembly, the kind of orators they are, the way some of them can rap, the accolades they win in sports and the talent they are endowed with make you swell with pride as they go on to become highly successful professionals. It is gratifying to see them return to their alma mater as completely transformed individuals. We have the power to transform lives. Are you willing to extend a helping hand? You can change the destiny of a generation. Play the role of a creator in the lives of His creations, and you will be blessed!

'Full many a gem of purest ray serene,
  The dark unfathom'd caves of ocean bear:
Full many a flow'r is born to blush unseen,
  And waste its sweetness on the desert air.'

—Thomas Gray

Creating a Better World

All men
Are not born equal,
But a kind heart
Can make a difference.

A pat, a nudge, a smile
Is what they need sometimes,
But the challenges of life
Are more than you can surmise.

Charity keeps
A poor man poor.
Education is what
Takes them far for sure.

A kind soul
Extending a helping hand
Is all they need
To transcend their background.

Self-motivated and focused,
Promising and talented they are.
A great destiny awaits them
If their life can be steered.

Come forward and help
The downtrodden and the needy.
With a heart that beats in empathy,
Become the architect of society!

Swachh Bharat: Taking pride in keeping the campus clean

Dare to be Different

'Educating the mind without educating the heart is no education at all.'

—Aristotle

My friend happily shared his nephew's incredible achievement in the NEET exam, in which he scored a perfect 720/720, thereby creating history! The celebrations went on for days. It was a proud and jubilant moment for the boy and his parents. In his interview, the boy said that he studied for 15 hours every day for two years, but what impressed me most was when he said he meditated every day. Meditation would have given him the energy, focus, mindfulness, willpower, a powerful mind and everything required to crack the exam.

We educationists naturally tend to focus only on academics. I agree that parents also send their children to a school based on the results they produce in the board exam. However, if we can work on the child's personality, we will actually be preparing them for life. Since mothers started working, they don't find the time to be with children. The family situation has shifted from a joint family to a nuclear one to both parents working. Having been in this field for three decades, I can see the cascading effect of today's family system, the exposure of children to inappropriate things, the influence of the West, the decline in value systems, the list goes on. All these have cumulatively triggered the need for schools to go beyond academics.

What kind of a society do we need? As we make an

important contribution towards national development, let us try and understand what goes into a child's holistic personality development. We know that academics alone will not empower a child. Some vital ingredients seem to be missing in a person in their basic role as an employee, employer, spouse, son or daughter, friend, citizen, etc. Do they have leadership qualities? Are they emotionally equanimous? Are they sensitive to their environment or to others' needs? Do they have integrity? Are they always complaining, or are they counting their blessings? Are they loving, grateful, responsible individuals? Is it enough just to score high marks and make the school proud? Are we preparing them for life?

'The best teachers are those who show you where to look, but don't tell you what to see.'

—Alexandra K. Trenfor

As much as we need to teach them various subjects, trigger their thought process, inculcate 21st-century skills in them, encourage them to be competitive and give them horizontal exposure, thus preparing them for a great professional life, achieving work–life balance requires a different kind of intelligence. Life and soft skills training given in school alone are insufficient to handle life's challenges. When there is a huge setback in life, will they have the resilience to face the challenge or will they crumble? Every time life pushes them down, will they get back up or will they be crestfallen? When they are faced with a situation in which their values are tested, will they make the right choice even if they stand to lose? Will they be a good Samaritan and look beyond me, mine and myself or live a selfish life? Will they be sensitive to others' needs and be willing to share? Will they be loving in their relationships or devoid of feelings? Will they be committed and sincere in their work, or will they be rolling stones? Will they be respectful or disrespectful towards others? Will they be a citizen the country can be proud of, or will they be traitors? Will they be role models or serve as a warning for others? These can be integrated into the school's curriculum. They are in school for most of their waking hours. Though it is the parents' responsibility to imbibe these qualities in a child, can we go the extra mile and adorn their personality? Let us not take the beaten path of academic excellence alone, which even parents desire. What is the point of an education that does not provide anything that sustains life? This thought made me delve deeper while framing the curriculum. We have several best practices at NSN. Through social contribution towards a noble cause every year, students are taught to look beyond themselves. Our students clean the school campus, house-wise, every Friday. Responsible citizenship is taught through this activity. Happy to Help is a volunteer group that ushers in the kindergarten students in the morning. They develop a helping nature. The Good Finders badge is given to students who write something good about someone every day; thus, we teach them to find goodness in the world. An Honesty Period has been introduced wherein if a class is not monitored when a teacher is on leave, students are expected to maintain discipline and complete their classwork. This helps develop their accountability and integrity. An Oath of Originality is taken every day to build their self-confidence. Students also make positive self-affirmations daily, which will ensure holistic growth and stay with them for the rest of their lives.

At NSN, our aim is to not only sharpen intellect but also broaden perspectives; widen the outlook and horizon; deepen vision and insight; strengthen human compassion, sympathy and understanding; and bring grace and charm into the minds of the students, thereby making them noble in proportion, high and steadfast in aim, wide and tolerant in outlook, beneficent in intention, and respectful of people's personality, dignity and worth.

Let's break the stereotype, become pathbreakers and provide a truly holistic education. There is a dearth of humane people in this world. Let's move away from the ordinary and create extraordinary citizens. That will be our contribution to the nation. Come, let's dare to be different.

'Education is not the learning of facts, but the training of the mind to think.'

—Albert Einstein

Be a Pathbreaker

Taking care of my body,
The gift I have received,
Is my responsibility,
Which I will never shirk.
That's what I learnt
As part of Physical Literacy,
For I am an NSNite.

Doing what everybody does
Is not how I live.
I question
My action, I reflect on
The right and wrong of it
As part of Moral Development,
For I am an NSNite.

Looking around and admiring
The beauty around me,
I immerse, I dissolve, I soak
In nature, in art and everything beautiful.
I have learnt to pause
As someone with a taste for aesthetics,
For I am an NSNite.

I care for my Motherland,
Which has given me this life.
I will make it very big
And make my country proud.

It is the cradle of human civilization.
I will be a responsible citizen,
For I am an NSNite.

Being calm and composed
Is what gives you happiness.
It is a huge challenge
To remove the agitation.
Achieving emotional equanimity
Is my relentless goal,
For I am an NSNite.

Working and playing together
As a team member or leader
Makes game and work enjoyable.
Give and take is my policy.
Win-win in every situation.
People skills are what I have developed,
For I am an NSNite.

Deep within me
There is a tranquillity.
I experience joy and happiness.
I meditate…
It is the key to holistic growth.
Spirituality unlocks the best in me.
I am grateful to be an NSNite.

Why a Teacher has to be a Role Model

'The journey is to evolve from animal to man and to eventually reach the Divine.'

—mahātria Rā

In some people's presence, you experience happiness, peace, the willingness to let go, the excitement to begin anew, the eagerness to learn, and the diminishing of the ego. One such person for me is my spiritual guru. His mere presence is transformational. He lives like you and me but says that there is a higher dimension to life that should not be missed. It will help us think and operate on a higher level. The teacher was explaining how man is made up of five different personalities and how peak performance cannot be achieved without growing in all five dimensions, namely, physical, mental, intellectual, emotional and spiritual. He believes that an ounce of practice is worth tons of preaching.

After the *satsang*, I was in a mood to reflect. If the mere presence of my spiritual guru can transform me, then a teacher should be able to have such an impact on the students. All of us seekers are adults, and it takes considerable time to transform an adult. It is much easier to influence children because they are more receptive. They observe and absorb. Children observe all our actions and absorb the learnings. We must be cautious in what we do and say, which is a humongous responsibility for a teacher. The moment we decide to become a teacher, we need to first get our being right with regards to all five dimensions, just as how a mother needs to prepare herself and create the right environment for her unborn child.

'A teacher affects eternity; she can never tell where her influence stops.'

—Henry Adams

This statement hit me hard when I decided to become an educationist. Thousands of students in the school had to be guided. I was not a perfect role model. I first had to get my actions right in all aspects. How disciplined was I? I had to take stock of my value system. What positive qualities did I possess? Could I lead them by example? Many such pertinent questions crossed my mind. I reflected on each one of them. Where was I, and where should I be? I decided that I would work on each of these and make myself worthy of the chair I occupied.

An educationist has to be responsible enough to take ownership of their actions. The first quality we need to imbibe is integrity, that is, to always be true to ourselves and to do the right thing even when we are not being watched. We cannot quantify the impact we have on our students, but it manifests in their lives. We are preparing students for life and not just for exams.

It was not an easy task, but I was clear about transforming myself in a way I would be proud of and also being able to lead others by example. Children learn more from what they see than from what they hear. Educationists have a huge responsibility to be role models to the younger generation. As Dr Kalam said, 'My life will be my message to my students.'

Be it our value system, the discipline with which we live our life, our behaviour, the language we use or the tone of our voice, everything has a message for our students. These are as important as preparing for class, delivering the concept or updating our knowledge.

As teachers, we should always remember that we are not only imparting knowledge to students but also moulding them to be responsible citizens, compassionate human beings and disciplined individuals who are the future of our nation. We are also mentors in that sense.

Teaching is a calling. A teacher has the power to influence their students. They can earn students' respect by the way they carry themself. They should not only be an inspiring teacher but also a person worthy of emulation. A teacher has to be mindful of their conduct and character. A teacher shapes a nation's destiny. I look forward to meeting such inspiring personalities. If you have one such person in your school, I would love to meet them. Let us become one such teacher, touch lives and make a difference!

The Being and Becoming of a Teacher

A sound mind in a sound body
Is what I believe
And practice.
Keeping myself
Healthy and fit.
Yes, I am a teacher.

I consciously strive
To walk my talk,
To be a role model
To the ones I teach.
I do not preach.
Yes, I am a teacher.

Training the mind,
Giving it a direction,
Setting a goal,
Being futuristic
Is the need.
Yes, I am a teacher.

Emotions galore,
I seep into the positive.
Attaining emotional equanimity,
My heart beats in gratitude
For all the blessings.
Yes, I am a teacher.

Aligned in thought and action,
Consistent in effort,
Growing in all dimensions,
Physical, mental, intellectual,
Emotional and spiritual,
This is how I wish to be,
For I am a nation builder.

The Demands of Your Role

Life was very simple when I was a child. The school was just a home away from home. Teaching was not complicated. I don't remember teachers having any behavioural issues with students in class. Some teachers were very friendly. There was some innocence in us. All our conversations with our friends used to be age-appropriate. Life was all about school, friends, cousins, studies, festivals, movies, and nothing else. It was simple. Most of our mothers were homemakers and took good care of us children. All habits and values were inculcated very early in life. Each family followed their own culture and tradition. Neighbours knew each other, and the whole street was like one big family. Parents used to reprimand others' children too. We don't live in such a world anymore.

When I joined this profession almost three decades ago, the situation was a far cry from what it is today. I am sure you will agree with me that distractions were less and children were more innocent because of their limited exposure to inappropriate things. Nowadays teachers have to deal with a totally different scenario, which is very challenging for them. There is a knowledge explosion, and they have to compete with all the distractions in children's lives and get their attention in a forty-minute period when their attention span is shrinking fast. The influence of Western culture is high; value systems have changed, and as both parents are working, they are unable to invest quality time with their children. In some cases, children are alone at home till the parents return from work. So there is no adult at home to monitor them. With the advent of social media and gadgets children use for playing games, watching videos, listening to songs, chatting with friends, and browsing sites, there is sensory overload; the mind is often filled with a thousand thoughts, which makes it chaotic. Consequently, children are unable to think with clarity. What is easy takes predominance over what is right. Many activities they indulge in are pleasure-driven, and low self-esteem and poor self-image drive them to choose the wrong crowd.

I am sure you will agree with me that all of these and much more have added responsibilities for an educationist as well as a teacher. Just as parenting has become a learnt trait, a teacher has to equip themself with skills needed to handle a heterogeneous class. They have to watch out for the students' behaviour and deliver the content in a most remarkable manner. Some students in every class are well-informed and knowledgeable, so a teacher has to prepare extremely well, be clear about the expected learning outcomes, be adept at using technology and certainly be good at student engagement. Students tend to respect only those whom they can look up to. So be well informed about the latest trends in teaching, the evolution of technology, advancements in science, innovations, etc. Because our schools are accredited by the National Accreditation Board for Education and Training (NABET), there is continuous improvement in all our processes, for which frequent feedback is taken from all stakeholders.

'Put the cause of men above the needs of man.'

—mahātria Rā

Furthermore, a small spark, if overlooked, can become a forest fire. This is true of students' behaviour as well. If we do not correct them when they are wrong, it will have an adverse impact on their adult life. Many a time we get so busy with completing the syllabus, meeting deadlines, organizing programmes, attending workshops and preparing question papers and lesson plans that we sometimes overlook children's behaviour. Some of us also get tired of correcting and lose interest in counselling students. Can we step up our influence and expand our reach? Children need our support much more than before.

> 'Good becomes best in the hands of right leadership.'
>
> —mahātria Rā

You must have experienced this as well. We cannot preach to this generation. Providing the right environment is the key. If we can model our behaviour and conduct, it will take care of the students' behaviour. The school environment facilitates a lot of subliminal learning. Hence, it has to be very positive. Teachers create the school climate and culture. At NSN, we strive to provide a child-friendly, threat-free learning environment. Needless to say, the school ecosystem has to be one where a child is nurtured with care and grows up to be a well-rounded individual. I am sure each of you is doing it your way.

We need to talk long enough to transform the young minds. Only teachers can make this happen. Every other day, the teacher can make it a practice to end their class with a five-minute talk with the students, sharing their personal growth experiences. The teacher can also tell them that they are vulnerable at times. This will put the students at ease, much more than when we talk to them in a holier-than-thou manner. They will be able to relate to us better. We need to go over to the child and bring them towards us. We cannot call them from where we stand and expect them to respond to our call. This is the stance I have taken with children. We can certainly create magic!

> 'Let us dream, and on the sheer strength of our dreams, let us get the world to stand up.'
>
> —mahātria Rā

Walk the Extra Mile

I gently breeze
into the school
With a promise
To make a difference
To the ones I teach.

They are a handful,
A heterogeneous group,
But I know that
Variety is
The spice of life.

Attitude, skill and knowledge
I need to possess.
With loving firmness
And a heart full of kindness
I care for them.

Teaching and counselling
Is what they need.
They live out of
Pain and pleasure
And not right and wrong.

As a teacher and mentor,
I need to empower
The fragile minds
Who need my support
To balance life.

A spark overlooked
Can create havoc.
Ever vigilant
I need to be
To nip it in the bud.

My love and kindness
Are a fuel
That nourishes them.
Anger and rudeness
Affect them.

Patience is the hallmark
Of a teacher.
A gentle approach
Works like magic
In transforming them.

I am defined
By my quality and ability.
I am in demand
To touch lives
And make a difference.
I always walk the extra mile.

Taking an oath to be a teacher who inspires

Empowering Mentors

In the great epic, *Mahabharata*, Ekalavya held Dronacharya in great reverence as his teacher and practised archery with his statue as his guide. That was how highly he regarded Dronacharya, who was worthy of worship. Arjuna was Drona's favourite student and was considered the best archer. However, in the battle of Kurukshetra, we all know that in spite of being a renowned archer, Arjuna was unwilling to fight. He became despondent. He needed Krishna to restore his confidence and faith in himself and convince him to fight the war of righteousness through the eighteen chapters of the *Bhagavad Gita*.

Similarly, in a modern-day school, students need a teacher to impart knowledge and a mentor to mould them. In short, they need a Drona and a Krishna in their life. Knowledge and character are equally important. Today students have a lot of exposure to right and wrong. They could be a teacher's agony or their delight. A teacher has to work in the right direction to strike a balance between the two roles, that of a subject teacher and a mentor, who moulds the character of the student. I cannot boast of having many teachers who have achieved cultural alignment. I guess many of us can say the same. Each school has its own culture, and only if teachers continue to work in one place will they be able to immerse themselves in the school's culture. We no longer have many teachers who have completed twenty-five years of service in one school. Even 10 years of continuous service has become rare. There are various reasons for this.

Now, how do we align them with the school culture? There is no sure-fire way to get it right. I am sure you are also trying different methods. We don't know what will click. We keep trying year after year, not knowing which method will work. One practice we have at NSN is taking the Oath for Teachers, written by Dr Kalam. All of us assemble in a spacious room that can accommodate all teachers and read the oath from the card together.

Eleven-point Oath for Teachers:

1. First and foremost, I will love teaching. Teaching will be my soul.
2. I realize that I am responsible for shaping not just students but also ignited youth, who are the most powerful resources on earth. I will be committed to the great mission of teaching.
3. As a teacher, it will give me great happiness if I can transform an average student of the class to perform exceedingly well.
4. All my actions with my students will be with kindness and affection like a mother, sister, father or brother.
5. I will organize and conduct my life in such a way that my life is a message for my students.
6. I will encourage my students to ask questions and develop the spirit of enquiry so that they blossom into creative enlightened citizens.
7. I will treat all the students equally and will not support any differentiation on account of religion, community or language.
8. I will continuously build capacities in teaching so that I can impart quality education to my students.
9. I will consider myself to be a great teacher only when I am capable of elevating the average student to a high performance. I will always celebrate the success of my students.
10. I realize that by being a teacher, I am making an important contribution to the efforts of national development.
11. I will constantly endeavour to fill my mind with great thoughts and spread nobility in thought and action among my students.

Every day, when we read it, the values get embedded in our minds and become a memory. A self-affirmation made daily helps us move closer to what we desire to become. One point could be discussed at a time before we leave for our respective classes. This has been a practice at NSN for several years. I also share the values of infinitheism with the teachers during the morning oath. Its wisdom is put up outside every room in the school so that it aids everyone's subliminal learning. Teachers are our greatest assets. The strength of all our schools is our teaching staff. If they are empowered, they will in turn empower the students. We try to get their thought process right. Each one has had a different upbringing, but all of them are required to be in tune with the school's vision and give students the right direction.

How do we inculcate the school's culture in students? Maybe you have a different system in your school, which I would love to hear about. One of the ways I have understood is through role modelling. I believe that if all of us can get our actions right, we will be able to influence the student community. I am sure this is a challenge we all face, but the intensity may vary. Where there are children, challenges are bound to exist. So we need to be highly equipped. Moral policing keeps happening in all our schools. To arrive at a common school culture, we may need to communicate with teachers repeatedly to align themselves to the school culture. At NSN, we get the student counsellor to address teachers on topics that are relevant at their level to sensitize them to students' needs. These counselling sessions are conducted periodically. We also conduct workshops for them on visioning, culture, empathy, etc.

Even though every school may have a counselling cell, they may not have a process of empowering teachers with the knowledge of counselling, right? It will come in handy. Students will respect them more with the way they handle their issues. All of us invest a lot in continuous professional development. Focussing on achieving high academic standards and many other factors that affect the school ecosystem will greatly help us. Every staff meeting I conduct is a transfer of energy, which helps bring a paradigm shift in teachers' attitudes. Building a school culture is an ongoing endeavour, but if senior teachers and students can set the right example, it will make our work a lot easier. The ones who can lead from the front can be recognized as change agents. Besides, the Pareto principle states that only 20% of people do 80% of the work. By motivating and acknowledging the top 20%, we can slowly change the school culture. We all understand that this will be our journey in education. Empowering mentors will be our priority, which will help us empower students and the nation at large. I would love to hear from you about how else you empower your teachers. Let us all come together and create a better world.

Teacher Empowerment

A nation
Is as developed
As its citizens.
The teacher
Shapes the destiny
Of the nation.

Every school
Should have
A proud line of teachers
Who are called
Change agents
Who impact society.

Capacity building,
Workshops and training programmes
Enhance their competence,
But inner engineering
Creates a paradigm shift
In their attitude and approach.

Every teacher
Should feel a connect
with the students.
That is when
They, too, will respond
With love and willingness.

Teacher empowerment
Should be the goal
Of every institution.
Setting the right environment
Will create the passion
To nurture students
For the nation.

Aligning the mind, body and soul through non-doing

An Overhaul

'He's still working on me
To make me what I need to be
It took Him just a week
To make the Moon and Stars
The Sun and the Earth and Jupiter and Mars
How loving and patient He must be
'Cause He's still workin' on me'

—The Hemphills

I was sitting at a spiritual retreat and praying to the Lord to clean me from the inside so that I would have purity in my thoughts and feelings. I heard my spiritual guru play the above song, conveying a strong message to me that cleaning the bottle from the inside is not a one-time job; it has to keep happening, just as how we bathe and brush our teeth every day, sometimes twice. It is an ongoing process. Tears were trickling down my cheeks because I knew that my guru understood my silent request; the song was answering my inner plea. It was once again a validation of who He was. I instantly thanked God for the beautiful life I was living through His teachings and wisdom. We need someone to help navigate our lives, to be a radar to prevent us from hitting a wall and bleeding, a rudder to keep changing the direction of our life, to propel us from complacency, accelerate our lives, open and expand our minds like a parachute, and transcend our shortcomings like a rocket that goes beyond the pull of gravity.

'Never underestimate the power of a small group of committed people to change the world. In fact, it is the only thing that ever has.'

—Margaret Mead

Every role we play in life demands that we possess certain core qualities and competencies so that we live a meaningful life. If we work towards it, we can bring quality into our lives. I see myself as a nation-builder. I thought that if I got my thinking right, I could mould the younger generation. Spirituality helps us know ourselves better, discover ourselves and bring out the goodness within us. We must learn to overcome the animal within us and grow in divine proportions. This is a continuous journey. Unless we are mindful and alert, we will not know when we are wrong. The constant correction allows us to rewire our thought processes. The mind of the man is the man. If the mind becomes powerful, we will be led in the right direction by our intellect. Else we will be led by pain and pleasure. We can contribute to the evolution of a better world if we, as educationists, have divine qualities. This has been my personal experience. Let us be that small group of selfless and determined souls who can change the world. Let us all give ourselves to the cause of education.

My spiritual growth helped me put the cause of man above the needs of man and become selfless. Meditating every day without fail transformed everything about my life. Today, my past looks like somebody else's past. My mind was so cluttered earlier. Fifteen years of meditation, starting with 11 minutes and eventually progressing to 1 hour, has changed my thought process, perspective, outlook, attitude, relationships, etc. Moreover, my spiritual connection has played a major role in enhancing the quality of my life. The importance of a healthy body was often reiterated. Yoga and going to the gym are part of my life, as is eating healthy food. There has been a drastic change in my lifestyle. Having developed a strong mind, I am able to embrace what is right and drop what is wrong, thus adopting healthy and right habits. A sound mind in a sound body is a prerequisite for a leader.

I invite you to experience a life of peace and harmony. You will not barter it for anything in life. To be able to say that life is beautiful, to be calm during adversity, not to become disturbed, not to hold ill-will against anyone, to count your blessings, to understand that starvation for love ceases only by giving love, to feel grateful for every heartbeat, to experience exponential growth, to achieve dynamism, to ensure that your life is right even when things are not going right, to live a fulfilling and holistic life, to always be full of energy and many more such qualities have become part of me. I am sure it looks like a tall order, but we can certainly achieve it with a spiritual anchor in our lives. I can assure you that life will not be the same again.

We educationists deal with the many emotions of students, parents and the staff. We should ensure that we are not disturbed or saturated. This will be possible only if we achieve emotional equanimity. If our energy levels are high, we will be able to easily handle these things without getting affected. We will also be more empathetic and deal with all matters in the right way. Mastering our emotions is the key to successful leadership. Like the lily pad that is not affected by water droplets on its surface, we should be emotionally detached from the challenges we face and handle them with maturity. Thus, we can avoid being drained of energy. What we do in school may look simple to others, but only we know an educationist's humongous responsibility. So, let us all gear up to surpass the expectations of the world by creating world-class citizens by aligning our mind, body and soul.

Aligning the Mind, Body and Soul

The mind can make
A heaven out of hell
And a hell out of heaven.
What is your choice?
Depends on
The power of your mind.
Loving, forgiving, caring, sharing
Are qualities to acquire
To be a great blessing
To this world.

Eating healthy
And staying fit
Is the only way
For a seamless life
Of wellness and health.
Aches and pains
Can be done away
With a healthy lifestyle
And a disciplined routine,
A gift unto ourselves.

Finding the purpose
Is the journey.
Sitting in silence
Will deliver the answer.
Spiritual growth
One should aspire for.

In it, we rejoice in
The bounties of life.
Through it, we cleanse and align
Our mind, body and soul.

Empowering teachers through continuous professional development

Leading the Changemakers

Teachers' Day is a memorable occasion because students express their love and gratitude to their teachers and some of them, who have walked the extra mile or who have stretched beyond the call of duty, are felicitated for their contribution to the school. Some of them get recognized year after year. It is not the number of years that we have worked as teachers but our contribution to the student community. Some of them are nominated for an award given by other organizations. Those who received such awards come to see me with the award and certificate, smiling ear to ear, visibly happy with the honours they received.

I have been incessantly working on creating exemplary teachers who are aligned with the school's culture and ethos. Becoming a teacher is not only about one's competence and efficiency but also about getting many equations right. A teacher has to enter the school every morning with the intent to serve and to be of value. Being a custodian of the lives of growing children is like taking up the responsibility of creating a masterpiece, a wonder of the world. Our work has to be flawless. As a leader of an institution, you design the destiny of so many children.

Each of us has our own ways to empower the teachers.

We can reach out to children only through teachers. The school's vision gives us a direction. It helps us all work towards the same purpose. A session on the school's vision will help the teachers understand the true value, purpose, aim and objective through which a school walks on the trajectory of success. Because the NSN Group of Schools is accredited, we have process owners who induct the new recruits. The correspondent talks about the school's culture and ethos. It takes time to bring the teachers on the same page and get them to speak the same language because we understand that each teacher comes from a different background. We go through our phases of shock and disbelief when it comes to the behaviour of a few. The Pareto principle says that 80% of the work is done by 20% of employees in an organization. I am glad that more than 90% of our teachers are in sync with the school's culture and ethos. This creates a sound school environment. In fact, we call them mentors as it defines their role.

We are dealing with human emotions, be it teachers or students. For both, their family culture and environment have a bearing on their personality. It is not easy to create a change in adults but takes a lot of consistent effort to do so. All my friends in the field of education have so many tales of woe about their search for an inspiring teacher, who seems to be very rare these days. Initially, I found it very tough to accept the behaviour of a few teachers and their lack of commitment. I judged them and looked at them in a condescending manner because of their attitude towards their work. However, my spiritual connection helped me change the way I approached the issue. In fact, it changed my entire personality. I decided to change my perspective for my own peace as negativity will only lead to more negativity.

That was the beginning of the transformation.

A true leader was born. I was able to look up to myself. When I introduced a shift in my thought process, I was able to handle my role with grace and dignity. When there is alignment in our life, the energy percolates. We usually tend to focus more on our actions. I realized that the first step was to get my being right. I ensured that my life was a message for my teachers and students. Meditation helped me transform my being. With positive reinforcement, teachers also became accountable and started taking ownership of the students. We need to talk to the teachers long enough. Apart from the meetings conducted by the principals, I conduct a staff meeting every month. I empower them with powerful thoughts and wisdom.

The power of the man is the power of his mind. Working on their mind for a prolonged duration helped. The wisdom I shared with them during the morning oath also helped transform their thought process. NSN's best practices helped students and teachers. Whenever teachers went beyond the call of duty, a staff shout-out was sent to the teachers' group to appreciate them. When they committed a mistake, an observation was made and the teacher was asked to sign. This was done one-on-one and filed. No teacher is condemned; only their action is corrected. They know we care for them in the way we treat them.

Apart from capacity-building programmes, workshops, in-service training, etc., which empower them to become efficient and effective teachers, we work on helping them become the best versions of themselves. Teachers meditate for 11 minutes before they leave. Good health is also given importance. There is a practice called Weigh to Go. All the staff members should weigh themselves and check their blood pressure every Monday in the Wellness Room. It is noted in a register, which is maintained by the staff nurse. The nurse also conducts valuable sessions for the staff to address their health. Every teacher is prepared for holistic growth. Competitions are conducted amongst the staff of the four houses, and prizes are given. Teachers are also asked to either play a game, do yoga or Zumba, or walk in the playground for half an hour before going home.

Teachers are directed with loving firmness.

The most cherished day that we all look forward to is the staff excursion. There is a lot of fun and camaraderie on that day. We go to a resort and have cultural programmes and games. We eat together and break all barriers. Thus there is a personal touch, and a relationship is built. We insist on disciplined freedom. Back at school, we are thorough professionals. Once they understand what is expected of them, they become aligned. This goes a long way in creating a beautiful environment in school. The connection between the head of the institution and teachers is vital to fostering a healthy environment for students. I am always willing to learn from educationists, so NSN's growth has been through benchmarking. Learning from others for continued growth and improvement has brought us to where we are today. Thank you, friends!

'Awareness is the greatest agent for change.'

—Eckhart Tolle

The Change Agents

The teacher
Creates the weather
And the climate
Of a school.

She defines
The joy and happiness
The rise and fall
Of her students.

She needs
To be empowered.
She needs
To be guided.

Some know it all.
Some others do fall
From the pedestal
Of worshipful altar.

The higher the teacher reigns,
The deeper is the surrender.
Students emulate
The teacher's behaviour.

A school is not only
A temple of learning
But also
A temple of transformation.

Let's realize
That individual good
Is a by-product
Of serving a larger good.

When I give.
I will be given.
That's the truth
And the paradox of life.

Worry not
About yourself.
The Creator will bless you
For you serve His creation.

Love
Is a giving emotion.
Give yourself
To the point of saturation.

You have the power
To create.
You are the one
Who can resuscitate.

You are the angel
Who can cast
A magic spell
And revive.

Go all out
With no restraint.
You are the creator
Of a new world!

A Worthy Life

'Education is what remains after one has forgotten what one has learned in school.'

—Albert Einstein

A school is a place where students come from a wide cross-section of society and from various backgrounds and collaborate with each other. Every school strives to bring them all to a common platform, as they differ from each other in various ways. A school is a miniature society where a child learns the qualities of love, friendship, empathy, tolerance, acceptance, sharing, caring, cooperation and much more, which are necessary for a peaceful society. Understanding the need for an education, which will help the child live a balanced life and fit seamlessly into society, the school has designed a beautiful curriculum for the students studying at NSN.

They are sensitized to the feelings of others because ultimately, life boils down to relationships, whether personal or professional. Success in both roles is essential. Especially during their tween years (middle school), they tend to fight with each other frequently. So when a child is celebrating their birthday, five students in the class are asked to say something good about the child. This not only makes the birthday boy/girl feel good but also teaches the other five to look for goodness in others.

There is also a Good Finder's badge to channel their energy and to help them see goodness in others. As tweens are at an age when they are restless, get irritated quickly and fight with each other due to the onset of puberty, their attention is diverted with this badge. Slowly, finding goodness in others will become a habit. That's the idea behind giving such a badge. Wearing this badge makes them feel proud. The teacher asks them to write something good about someone every day in the school handbook and show it to them. Students who write consistently during the month get a badge. Initially, they write consistently at least for the sake of the badge. Slowly, it will change their outlook.

Children are encouraged to look around them to see if anybody needs their help. They should not always expect to be served; rather, they should be ready to serve others. To inculcate the habit of helping others, we initiated the Happy to Help group. Students are assigned duties at the school gate in the morning. It is such a pleasurable sight to see these students, especially boys, usher in the kindergarten students. They bring them in with a lot of care. Some of them literally carry these children to class and pacify the ones who are crying. When such responsibilities are given to children, they automatically become responsible and duty-conscious individuals.

The Karuna Club instils compassion in children through various activities so that they do not entertain any violent thoughts. Peace must prevail at all costs. Brotherhood, love and peaceful coexistence should be the dominant thoughts. This will help preserve the environment and ensure a balance in the ecosystem.

We want our students to think big and not aim for ordinary goals. They should make their country proud. Scientists have emerged, with one of them receiving the Shanti Swarup Bhatnagar Award, the highest award for outstanding research in science and technology in India; another received the Pradhan Mantri Rashtriya Bal Puraskar; yet another student set a new Guinness World Record; and some have founded NGOs. Students have taken new paths in life, and one of them, a Vedic speaker, is followed by even the prime minister of the country on X (formerly Twitter).

This is the diversity of their achievements and their contributions to the country.

By inculcating values in them through suitable experiences, the school gradually trains their mind to live a life they can always feel proud of. Growing in our own eyes is the toughest but most important task. We need to feel proud of ourselves first. That's the individual we want every NSNite to become by making their life worth living. They should always aspire to live a worthy life! Value building is nation-building.

'One day your life will flash before your eyes. Make sure it is worth watching.'

—Gerard Way

Grow in Your Own Eyes

To be at peace
With the world,
Loving and caring
For every creation
Is the path I have chosen.
'So I practice *ahimsa*.'"

To do
All the good I can,
For all the people I can,
In all the ways I can,
At all the times I can.
'Thus, I will make my life count.'

Not mediocre
But an achiever
I will be.
Rising above
The ordinary,
'I will make my country proud.'

Living a worthy life,
Being a good Samaritan,
Touching lives
And making a difference
Is getting my being right.
'I will live to look up to myself.'

Post-pandemic Blues

'Every "today" is God's gift.
"Today" is God's way of telling you,
"You can start again..."
Make every day count.'

—mahātria Rā

Nature's fury has no boundaries. When it decides to retaliate, it brings unimaginable destruction. It comes with a vengeance. Be it hurricanes, tornadoes, tsunamis, earthquakes or the most recent Coronavirus, we are made to realize how small and vulnerable we are. Nevertheless, we have to get back up and start all over again. Coronavirus taught us that nothing is permanent, that everything is transient. The beauty is that people never fail to see the materialistic destruction around them. They keep ruing over it and feel the pain, but they never notice the inner shift in a person after the calamity. One such shift in personality occurred in children during the pandemic.

Everything changed for children. A virtual classroom was their day-to-day experience. Their school was within a desktop/laptop/mobile. They could neither meet friends physically nor go out to play. The virtual classes made them manipulative. They switched off the video, did not attend the virtual class, ate during the class, brought friends from other schools into the virtual class by sharing the link and essentially did everything that gave them pleasure but took them very far in the wrong direction. It was a tough period for all. Parents were working from home, so they could not monitor their children. Some of them lost their near and dear ones, while many were neck deep in financial trouble as they had lost their jobs. Schools were finding it difficult to collect fees from parents. Many adjustments had to be made. Students also lost the discipline to do everything on time. They even sat in the virtual class without taking a bath. Lethargy set in.

Most of you will agree that it was the most challenging period in our profession. All the right habits we had inculcated in our students simply vanished. When children started returning to school, all of us had a tough time, right? The principal had to handle the staff as well as the students. Teachers had got used to teaching from the comforts of their homes and found it difficult to come to school on time. They lacked energy. To add to our woes, students had lost the goodness within them in terms of values and discipline. They also lost touch with studies, and a huge learning gap was staring at us. We had to work with them on their behaviour and habits. Wherever I went, every educationist complained. I, too, was part of it till I realized we need to focus on our circle of influence rather than our circle of concern. We then started working on solutions.

We took two years to bring back normalcy. I am sure all of you would have bounced back by now. All the efforts that we had put in over the years to groom the students were washed away by the pandemic. Nevertheless, I must say that we are fighters. If nothing else, the pandemic has made us stronger and more resolute. We decided to calm down the children first. Some of them were anxious and had an unknown fear. Girls in their early teens had attained puberty, and boys also showed the first signs of growth. They had seen each other two years before. With the physical changes, they felt awkward. The challenges their families faced also impacted them. We started with mass counselling, which helped the students come out with their problems and remove all the disturbances they had within them.

NSN's way of integrating spirituality with education came to our rescue. We always begin the day by asking students to sit in silence for 11 minutes. We build their self-confidence through the Oath of Originality, which they take every morning. A Tree of Joy is created wherein children express their thoughts on the theme for the month, which is related to the qualities to be imbibed in them. They also have the will power drive every month. The idea that it takes 21 days to form a habit originated from a book titled *Psycho-Cybernetics* by Maxwell Maltz. We try to inculcate the right thoughts and actions in them through this. These are a few of our best practices. By creating an environment high on energy and positive vibes, we are able to see a vast difference.

Regarding academics, we had to work on their listening, speaking, reading and writing skills for language and teach basic operations in mathematics. A lot of bridging had to be done. Although they have come a long way, we have much further to go in academics. In terms of children's psychological and emotional well-being, they have recovered and recouped very well. Today, none of us is discussing the post-pandemic blues. We are surging forward with new aspirations and renewed vigour. Didn't the pandemic make us all pause? Only schools with quality standards could survive. Let us all come together as a community; share our school's best practices, challenges and solutions; strengthen the power of educational institutions in the country; and pave the way for a new India!

Overcoming Challenges

Man has become invincible,
Exploring the universe,
Reaching the moon
And the sun.
Science and technology
Are innovating
Most and more!

Yet, man became powerless
In the presence
Of a virus,
Which caused great havoc
And ruined lives
When it emerged
In gigantic proportions.

Yes, the pandemic
Brought us all
To our knees.
Scared and unsure we were
Of seeing
One more day,
Another sunrise.

The whole world closed.
Life froze, and fear gripped.
Never before
Did we experience

An onslaught
Of this sort.

We had only questions to ask,
But no answers came forth.
Life went for a toss.
Everything changed.
The new normal began.
We lost
The human touch.

Leaders had to act,
Detaching from the experience,
Attaching to the process.
Create an environment
To restore normalcy,
To bring back the smile
And the feeling of belongingness.

Fear was replaced.
Trust took its place.
Confidence was built.
Tears were wiped.
Courage was created.
A better world emerged.
That's the power of a teacher!

Creating a bond between parents and children on Thanksgiving Day

Building Relationships

In India, the family is the smallest unit of society. What holds a family together is the love they have for each other. Family values are handed down to the children. The home environment is crucial to a growing child. The school houses children from different backgrounds. Having common ground for all helps a great deal, but we also know that a school has a heterogeneous group. So, the school is responsible for steering all of them in the right direction. It is a golden triangle. Teachers and parents have to come together for the students' welfare. Their outlook and approach have to be aligned, and there has to be a great deal of understanding between the school and parents. Unless we think along similar lines, we cannot contribute to their growth.

Parents have to choose the right school for their children. Enquire about the school's vision, culture, policies and philosophy before admitting the child. Once enrolled, they should not question the grammar of the place. There has to be implicit trust in the school's intentions. They need to joyfully participate in the child's education so that the child has a comfortable stay in school. Choosing a school that suits their child is most important because that will be a home away from home for them. The teacher has to be a parent in school. As heads of institutions, if we educate the parents by communicating long enough, we can bring them on the same page. It is important that our values are similar. This helps build a solid foundation upon which children can start their lives.

I remember meeting the mother of a student, who was a first-generation learner. She shared the values she inculcates in her children and how she contributes to making life comfortable for them because, being uneducated herself, she cannot help them in academics. One thing she told her children hit me hard. She told them that whatever they became in the future was because of the foundation laid by the school. So they should touch the floor of the school every day before entering the building as a mark of gratitude for the education they were receiving. It profoundly affected me. From then onwards, I touch the floor of NSN, whispering my gratitude to the Almighty by saying, 'Thank you, God, for choosing me as Thy instrument. I am truly blessed.' A valuable life lesson was imparted to me by an 'uneducated' mother!

Most parents are very supportive. They keenly monitor their children, take them to various classes after school, encourage them to join a sports academy or learn some art form and do what is required for their skill development and growth. They also instil values in them. However, there are exceptions as well. I find a huge difference in children's upbringing in some families where there is discord in the family or the mother goes to work. The lady in the house is highly stressed as she has to manage household chores as well as her professional work. This is also the case with fathers. Workplace stress or family issues affect them emotionally. Refined behaviour is uncommon. Screaming and yelling, speaking disrespectfully and rudely to the school staff to assert their rights, humiliating and insulting them and having misplaced emotions have become widespread.

With the advent of social media, people have begun losing the social grace that defines the educated and cultured. For some, it seems to be their very nature! This is adversely affecting the children. The use of gadgets from a very early age is harming them. Their ability to read has considerably declined; their behaviour is so different; they have lost the beautiful smile on their faces; they don't interact much; and they live in their own world and seem absent from the real world. This is because parents do not spend quality time with them.

Many educationists have shared similar experiences with me. I see concern writ large on their faces.

The Reach Out Programme that we conduct at the beginning of every academic year helps us reach out to parents to convey what the school expects from them and what they can expect from the school. We also talk about the values that we need to instil in children and how parents should spend quality time with them. Some parents have told us that this programme has transformed them. By and large, the parents are aligned with NSN's values. We have earned their support, goodwill and cooperation!

Children are the message we send to the future that we may not live to see. Nevertheless, we can continue to live through our children and the values we inculcate in them. Like the Chinese bamboo tree that takes five years to show signs of growth but shoots up to a height of one hundred and fifty feet in the next three months, the values and discipline we inculcate in our children may not be evident immediately but will bear fruit in later years.

Growth and values are not taught; they are caught. Hence, parents have a humongous responsibility to live a life of values. Children should not see a disconnect between their thoughts and actions because they learn more from what they see than from what they hear. In short, children learn what they live. The environment in which they live grooms them. The family environment is our area of concern. We cannot do much to influence it. Talking to the parents, providing them with a counselling cell, etc., will help educate them to an extent. That is the best we can do.

Involving parents in some school activities, the PTA and School Management Committee will encourage and motivate them. We also use them as resource persons for guest lectures. Parents' talents can allow them to be judges for competitions. They can also be asked to train students in an area they are specialists in.

To a large extent, this will make them feel important and good. Some mothers have joined our school as teachers. Whenever there is a concern or feedback from parents, we call them and clarify things. If it is a complaint, we act on it and resolve it with a satisfactory note from the parent.

Children's Day is earmarked as Thanksgiving Day. Students are encouraged to give a letter of love and gratitude to their parents. This helps them bond. A cordial relationship between parents and the school is crucial for the child's emotional well-being. So we need to educate, involve and appreciate the parents, which will go a long way in fostering and building a beautiful relationship between them and the school.

To Love and to be Loved

With utmost joy, you cherished my birth.
For unbounded love and happiness
There was no dearth.
I felt your touch and care.
With me, you were always there.

Your life revolved around me.
In your hug, I dissolved.
I was the cynosure of your eyes.
You skipped a heartbeat
If you missed my voice.

I was the apple of your eyes,
The purpose of your life.
Ages and stages do bring changes,
And then I became a teen.
I know how I have been.

You have tolerated my tantrums.
You became my punching bag.
You withstood all my outbursts,
But you made sure
That I did not crumble.

You stand tall in your values,
Unwavering in your discipline,
Steadfast in your commitment,
Unconditional in your love.

You are the best gift of my life.

You are a university unto yourself,
A role model of a parent.
I need not seek elsewhere
For inspiration and motivation
As I am blessed with wonderful parents.

Mom and Dad, I must say,
You are my best friends,
A beacon of light,
A ray of hope,
The sunshine of my life!

Work–Life Balance

'Don't get so busy making a living that you forget to make a life.'

—Dolly Parton

In the battle of Kurukshetra, Arjuna became despondent and was not ready to fight the war even though he was the best warrior. Krishna had to convince him, 'If not for you, at least for the sake of the other kshatriyas, you need to fight the war. Fight, Arjuna, fight.' Krishna said that Arjuna would have to lead the others by fighting the war of righteousness. The eighteen chapters unfolded for the sake of Arjuna's transformation. Similarly, as heads of institutions, we need to lead others by showing them how we balance our work and personal lives.

Initially, I was reluctant to work because I wanted to be a homemaker, so it was a period of complaining and blaming others.

My heart would cry to be with my little son, and when I couldn't, I blamed everyone, not that it alleviated my pain or sorrow. It was resistance from my side. Anything you resist becomes a mental block, and you are unwilling to give yourself fully to your work. This happens when the going gets tough. Moreover, I was new to the field and had a lot of catching up to do. I used to carry my files home and work till late into the night after spending some quality time with my son. This went on for some years. I was always told not to take work home. I wished I didn't have to, but the workload was high. My son's education was my priority. So I would come home, sit with him and get him to prepare for his tests and complete his homework. He was my world. Nothing else mattered to me. I stopped watching television; I had no social life, and I did not attend weddings or functions. I only focused on school and my son. I used to go to school even during the holidays. As time passed, we started going on a vacation once a year.

My health took a beating with all the stress I underwent. Fortunately, I came in contact with my spiritual guru around 11 years after I started working. That was the beginning of my transformation and the blossoming of a beautiful life. For someone who was using the word stress generously, everything about my life changed. That word was dropped from my vocabulary. I stopped speaking a victim's language. Life started looking up. I began to understand the right way to live my life.

My guru always said, 'The power of the man is the power of his mind. The power of the mind is the power of the subconscious mind. The power of the subconscious mind is the power of the subconscious belief. The power of the subconscious belief is built by making and honouring commitments.' Say it, and do it.

What began small has now accelerated my maturity and life so much that it would have otherwise taken me decades to reach where I am, from a naïve, disturbed, confused, immature, emotional, impulsive, restless, stressed and pessimistic individual to a person who is living a life of holistic abundance. Touchwood! I have been in a beautiful space for the past 16 years. Meditation has become a vital part of my life. When a thought is released from the seat of silence, a mere wish becomes a command to the universe. I have begun attracting all my desires. Clarity of thought has emerged. I have stopped reacting. I started experiencing peace and harmony. There is no more struggle in life.

I am sure you delegate what others can do and do only what you can do. Developing a competent second line is key. A team is not only a group of competent people but also a group of compatible people. This will give you a lot of time to take the vision forward. I am burning with desire to contribute in a big way to revolutionize education. In this way, I am able to devote time to take the school forward. My time is invested in what is important but not urgent. The future of the school comes from here. That is how we got our schools accredited by the Quality Council of India. The way forward is by asking the question, 'What more, what else and what next?' By planning the work for the day and setting aside time for academics, administration and future planning, I am able to use my day productively.

I am good at swapping roles. I don't carry my work pressure home. When I am at home, I am only with my family.

I am a home bird. Because I am always in public life, I fiercely guard my privacy. I don't carry any of my personal issues to my workplace either. I practice detached attachment. Only when you get too close in a relationship do you get burned. I love my students just as I love my son. I realized that starvation for love ceases only by giving love. My heart beats for them. NSN is a cause. Because I am deeply attached to the cause, it has become my life's purpose. I breathe NSN; I eat NSN; I dream NSN; I live NSN. It is very difficult to explain this. I am helplessly in love with my work, which is actually a calling. Today, I beautifully and seamlessly manage my home and work. Neither of them can complain about not receiving my personal attention.

I go on family holidays at least thrice a year and travel more than that with my husband. When you enjoy what you do, work becomes your hobby and you don't feel you have worked for a single day. Planning, executing and achieving are all important. NSN is experiencing exponential growth. I don't limit myself to one role. I have become relentless. Someone who once shed tears upon becoming a professional is now happily doing this, that and that too!

Most importantly, it is true that when you are passionate

about whatever you do, you will be able to bring about work–life balance and join the exclusive club of peaceful and happy beings. Your ability to juggle umpteen things at a time will also increase, and you will make the world exclaim, 'It's amazing!'

'When you find work
In which your heart can express itself,
You find happiness in it.
It can no more be called work.'

—mahātria Rā

Tightrope Walk

Life is a dicey game
For those who are not aware
Of the nuances, the tricks and the order
Of the game.

Life is an art
That some have knowledge of.
While some learn and cultivate,
Not all can master it.

Time is a great resource.
Use it wisely.
Where your time goes,
There your future comes.

If your heart is
Where your work is,
Everything that you do
Will seem divine.

Riding a wave of joy
That is seemingly eternal,
Experiencing peace and harmony
Are but a matter of balance.

Passion brings commitment,
Enjoyment and enrichment.
Nothing will seem like a burden
When the options are open.

Prioritize and plan
The life you desire.
Set your boundaries,
And do away with all worries.

Life will be a dance,
Life will be a song,
Life will be a celebration
If you learn to balance.

Work-life balance
is a tightrope walk.
You can do this and that
If you have mastered it all.

Teaching coping strategies to students via counselling sessions

Anger Management

When the little child is playing happily all by himself, nobody in the family notices them, but when they fall or get hurt, everybody in the family rallies around and gives them attention. Similarly, when a child is forbidden from doing something or when they do something wrong, the family members immediately pay attention. The child understands that the only way to get attention is to do something forbidden or wrong. When a child falls, we hit the floor to console the child. The child understands this as blaming the floor. So, every time the child falls, the floor is blamed. The message conveyed to the child is that they can blame someone else for the mistakes they commit.

> 'When good behaviour is recognized and rewarded, it will be repeated.'
>
> —mahātria Rā

When they grow up, they use these tools to get attention. They also believe that they can indulge in blame game. This is a two-minute-noodles generation that wants everything in a jiffy. Children get angry due to many reasons, but these reasons must be addressed in childhood. Childhood trauma, pampering, inferiority or superiority complex, attention deficit hyperactivity disorder (ADHD), the home environment and discord in the family, to name a few, could trigger anger. It not only affects their day-to-day life but also their relationships. Nobody would want to be around an angry person.

Students fighting with each other is a common sight, but when a streak of violence is seen in a particular student, we go deep into the issue to analyse the behavioural pattern and not just condemn or brand the child. Parents are also called and spoken to in order to understand the child better. It would be interesting to know how each school addresses anger management. We must upgrade our skills to handle students' emotions. Students are a work in progress. There is always a better way to do things. If teachers are trained to be counsellors, especially from classes VI–XII, it would be a great help. They would be equipped to handle the students, not simply brand or judge them.

At NSN, the student counsellor makes an annual plan to conduct sessions for students, parents and teachers. Anger management is one such session, which is conducted to educate students on the ill effects of destructive anger and its consequences on the individual, family, friends, and colleagues in the workplace and society in general. Students are taught how to assertively control their anger without hurting themselves or others and by addressing its root cause. Students learn how anger affects them physically, psychologically and also their social life. They are taught techniques for developing healthy stress management, effectively communicating their emotions and maintaining a healthier lifestyle.

Parents and teachers are briefed on how to handle angry young kids. They have to come together to support the child and help them overcome their negative emotions.

We ask students to identify triggers and warning signals, talk to someone they trust, try breathing exercises, move away from the situation, walk every day or change their thinking. Keeping a journal to track their anger triggers, engaging in mindfulness and relaxation exercises, seeking professional help or celebrating the times they could overcome their anger will all help. Every morning, students practice mindfulness in school. They can also seek help from the counsellors. They are made to understand that their anger affects them first as it secretes acid into their body. Once they understand the futility of getting angry, they will slowly work on reducing it.

Students don't realize that we achieve nothing by getting angry. We only lose our peace of mind. Gautama Buddha said, 'Holding on to anger is like grasping a hot coal with the intent of throwing it at someone else; you are the one who gets burned. You will not be punished for your anger; you will be punished by your anger.'

The present generation faces immense peer pressure. Don't you think students need an outlet for all the pressure that builds up? Yoga and meditation will help keep them calm. Exercise is a good way to relax. Students should be encouraged to talk about their emotions, right from when they are at the primary level, and how they feel every day. Sports are a great way to let off steam and will teach them many vital life lessons. Music, dance, painting and other art forms are also therapeutic and healing. For some, they are meditative. They should be initiated into one of these from childhood. They should not be engaging only in studies. They should have some creative pastimes as well. Developing a hobby will help them relax.

All this can start early in life. Diverting their attention to something else will also help. Achieving emotional balance is crucial; otherwise, it will ruin their life. They need a conducive environment at home. Parents and teachers should model their behaviour. If the adults in their lives are emotionally balanced, it will significantly help the child. The environment can make a huge difference to a child's emotions. A relationship hinges on a person's emotional well-being. Emotional maturity and balance can be achieved only by constantly working on them. We have a huge responsibility to bring stability to our students' lives. I am sure your timely intervention transformed the lives of many such students.

Thus, you became a catalyst who brought about the vital change required in the student community, reiterating the significance of a true teacher. More power to you!

Volcanic Eruptions

In the animal world
Where might is right,
Life is driven
By pain and pleasure.

The mind can create
A heaven out of hell
Or a hell out of heaven
For each of us.

We can be
A master or a slave
To our emotions.
What is your choice?

Either you control
Or you succumb
To your emotions.
Choose your way.

The volcano erupts
In all its fury.
The hurricane destroys everything
In its way.

The tsunami
And the earthquake,
The floods and the drought
Are a curse to man.

Such is the bane
Of anger.
All relationships lost,
Peace passes away.

An angry man
Can see no reason.
He is consumed
By his emotions.

Losing control
Of the situation,
Losing track
Of his mind.

Just pause…
Just be…
Just think…
Angry you will not be.

The emergence of a new school

Beyond the Comfort Zone

'Growth needs transformation;
Transformation needs change;
Change needs transition
And transitions are never comfortable.'

—mahātria Rā

Whenever I have done something, my mind has always focused on 'what' I want to do. The 'how' has always miraculously unfolded. We wanted to celebrate the first anniversary of infinitheism in 2012 by planting 1,111 saplings in the neighbourhood. A plan was made, and the strategies were worked out. Many asked how I would get the students of NSN to walk around the streets and plant these saplings, who would make the pit, from where we would source the saplings, if the tree guards would be taken away by someone who wanted to make money by selling them, if the cattle would graze on these plants, and other such questions. My only answer to all these questions was, 'We will do it and show.' We achieved the feat in just nine days! Today, 12 years later, we can see the trees lining all the avenues.

Was it easy to do this? Definitely not. However, we wanted to leave behind a legacy. We wanted to contribute to our environment. We had to undergo some discomfort to achieve our goal. If we wish to go beyond me, mine and myself, we should be willing to embrace some discomfort. Nothing great can be achieved by staying in our comfort zone.

Once, when we wanted to take some of our students on a trip to Dubai, many who wished to come did not have their passports.

I didn't want to disappoint them, so I decided to arrange to apply for their passport. It looked like a tall order, but I wanted to help them. I was dissuaded from taking up the challenge of procuring passports for thirty-five students. Nevertheless, I went ahead. I worked on the logistics, and lo and behold, everyone received their passports in time! Now, I am wondering how all this materialized. I realize that in all these situations, I was willing to go beyond the imaginary finishing line.

'The bounties of life are always beyond the imaginary finishing line.'

—mahātria Rā

During a conversation with a good friend of mine, she mentioned that her dad was asking her to start a new business. She happened to tell him how I was starting a new school at the age of sixty-one. That was when it struck me that I had crossed sixty years and was venturing into a new school, which would need all my energy. I never even thought about my age when we planned to buy land for another school. Yes, I was much younger when we were scouting for land. By the time we found suitable land, purchased it, came up with a plan and got all the approvals, it took us almost six years, as the pandemic in 2020 caused a further delay.

When I am doing something, I just focus on the process and nothing else. I was shaken for a moment when I heard what my friend said. She most probably will not venture into anything new at my age.

'Growth is nothing but going from lesser comfort to higher comfort through uncomfortable transition.'

—mahātria Rā

I well know that I have to start all over again by establishing a new school. The last school we started was in 2012. It certainly needs a lot of courage, but I am willing to stretch myself beyond my comfort zone. I already have two schools (NSN Chromepet and NSN Memorial) to visit every day. I would have to visit the third school (NSN Kundrathur), too, but if I have to reach out to more students, this is one way forward. I have already created a strong second line, and they, in turn, are working on the third line of leadership. I have transformed from a person who was micromanaging the school to a person who is working at the macro level. I had to work relentlessly to reach here. Creating leaders takes time.

The pandemic threw us all out of gear. Teachers, who had, till then, resisted using technology in class, were forced to teach classes online when schools became virtual. First, it was about using technology and taking classes. The second was learning to use the various features. The third was to teach from home, which, in their minds, is a place of rest. Some teachers were good with technology. They mentored and supported other teachers and helped them overcome their fears. How teachers and the school came out of this challenging situation is a miracle. Here again, it was going beyond our comfort zones.

Similarly, when the schools decided to go for accreditation, all the staff had to be trained. Processes, systems and documentation are all part of the NABET accreditation. All of us were grappling with the situation. Today, we have come a long way in terms of renewing our perspective, mindset and the way we work. The focus is on continual improvement and benchmarking. The school has grown exponentially ever since and transitioned from a person-driven organization to a system-driven one.

With the advent of social media, people's reading habits have drastically dwindled. Only readers become leaders. Developing a nation of readers is a dream. Young student authors are already showing their talent at NSN.

This movement should be led by teachers. I am thinking of starting a Reading Club for teachers. They can be divided into groups and asked to read a few chapters of a book. They can share what they have read so that everyone will know the content of the book and be inspired to read the remaining chapters. Their mind will expand, and their perspectives may change. Initially, there may be some resistance, but eventually, they will build a habit of reading. We will begin with one book a term or three books a year. I need not elaborate on the benefits of reading to educators. Please share what you do to inculcate a habit of reading in teachers. Right now, they are in their comfort zone.

Life will throw us into an uncomfortable transition when we are least prepared. Actually, we can never be sufficiently prepared for life's exams. It comes without prior notice. We believe the easiest thing to do is quit. This is a mindset we need to change. Irrespective of the situation or the environment not being conducive, we need to persist. Life is all about acceptance and the willingness to move on. We can face anything if we are willing to go through uncomfortable transitions. Legendary people always undergo uncomfortable transitions and reach a new comfort zone. We always grow during life's uncomfortable transitions. We tend to get comfortable where we are, but we are much more than what we think we are. Explore all the possibilities. We can go as far as we can see. When we reach there He will show us the further path.

'Every finishing line
Is a new starting line.'

—mahātria Rā

Get...Set...Go!

Every landmark
Was an effort.
The proficiency
They gained
Was an effort.
The greatness
They achieved
Was an effort.

Every glory
People enjoy,
Every milestone,
Every award,
Every victory,
Every achievement,
Every applause they received
Began with effort.

To move forward,
To set new records,
To climb high,
To revel and rejoice,
To win laurels,
To inspire others,
We need to be
Happily dissatisfied.

Keep aiming for more.
Reset your axis.
When you plateau,
Plan your next action
And execute
The right strategies.
Never be satisfied
Nor be contented.

Limitations are
In the mind.
Potentials are
Infinite.
Just decide
To be better
Than the best.
Your time, you invest.

Growth and change
Should be a constant.
You will discover
A new you.
Push yourself,
And a champion will be born.
Life's bounties are
Beyond the imaginary finishing line.

Building students' confidence through the oath of originality

Dented Self-image

'Beauty isn't about having a pretty face. It's about having a pretty mind, a pretty heart and a pretty soul.'

—Drake

People have always been fond of looking good. It is believed that Cleopatra, often depicted as 'beautiful', bathed in donkey's milk. This obsession with beauty has a flip side. It sometimes makes people narcissistic. It is important to look presentable and have a good personality, but one should not get obsessed with one's looks. Beauty is only skin deep.

Nowadays, a book is judged by its cover. You are first judged by your looks and only then probed about your subject knowledge when you attend an interview. Wear a personality till you become a well-known personality. Nobody would have ever judged Dr Kalam for his long hair because his achievements were far beyond that. So he was not commented upon but looked up to.

Some parents ignorantly nickname their children without realizing its impact on the child's psychology. Children are targeted for their skin colour, features, size, height, etc. Is any of these the child's fault? The child grows up with an inferiority complex and develops low self-esteem.

When a child is bullied at home, they go to school and take it out on their classmates by becoming violent or exhibiting misplaced emotions. In some cases, when we have received a complaint about a child's behaviour, probed deep into it and called the parents; we have discovered that one of the parents is either strict or has dented the child's self-image.

A child growing up with a dented self-image has to deal with many issues. They cannot maintain good relationships and will have a troubled life as an adult. Realizing this, I decided that when I had a child, I would transform myself to suit their needs. My personality changed to create a positive environment at home. My child was never exposed to any discord between his parents; he was never judged or labelled or branded; his looks were never discussed; he was made to feel special yet grounded. So he grew up with good self-esteem and self-worth.

At NSN, we address the parents through the Reach Out Programme regarding the importance of providing the right environment at home for children. We ask them to highlight the child's positive qualities and not keep talking about their negative behaviour. Parents can build the child's self-confidence by simply using words of praise every time the child does something right. Since I grew up with low self-esteem, I know that it hurts.

We also work with the students through our student counsellors. Students start becoming self-conscious and a little awkward when they are tweens. That's the time they attain puberty. There will be physiological changes in boys and girls. I am sure you also involve your counsellors to talk to students. They are asked to develop acceptance regarding their looks as it is an area of concern. They tend to compare themselves with what they see on social media. They need immense courage to say no to their peer group. To not be a part of a gang is very tough.

Self-love is very important. Unless they love themselves, they cannot accept themselves. They must be the first to appreciate themselves. To do so, we ask them to perform small good deeds by which they feel proud of themselves. Whatever their sore point may be, we should help them overcome it by sitting together and making a plan. Children should be taught to focus on what is important. They should constantly be told about the importance of feeling beautiful from within. Their inner beauty must be acknowledged and appreciated. This will help them feel good and not just look good. We need to work more on their 'being domain', that is, their core qualities.

All three stakeholders—the children, parents and teachers—are crucial in addressing this issue. Each one is addressed separately. Parents and teachers are guided on how to handle the child, and students are given tips on how to overcome criticism. The student counsellor evaluates their body image using an assessment tool. Poor body image results from peer pressure when they believe their friends look good but they don't. Social media has a huge influence on the younger generation.

Some of them seek attention by applying bold make-up and wearing revealing clothes. Parents are unaware of what they post on Instagram or Facebook.

They sometimes go to the extent of befriending strangers on social media platforms. They like anyone who gives them attention. This is the most dangerous part. Parents and teachers should wake up to this startling reality. Children should be able to take their parents into confidence. Gone are the days of maintaining respectful distance with parents. There has to be close rapport for parents to ensure that they don't lose their children.

Schools have a humongous responsibility to educate parents and empower teachers on these matters. Our main focus is to prepare students for life. How equipped are they to face life's challenges? Life is not all about marks but about having the necessary skills and the right attitude as well.

If like-minded educationists could come together and share their best practices, that would help enrich each other. The school has to be in constant touch with the parents. After all, children's mental well-being is as important as their physical well-being. So, at NSN, we make students take an oath of originality every morning to build their self-confidence, as follows:

'In the history of the world,
There has been nobody like me.
To the infinite of times to come,
There will be nobody like me,
And even today,
There is nobody like me.
I am rare;
I am unique;
I am original;
I am an NSNite.
I will make it very, very, very big in life.'

Body Shaming

Childhood was all play,
Fun and chatter.
We soiled
Our clothes,
Ate every damn thing,
Ran all over,
The place,
Clumsy and stupid
At times.

How we looked,
How we sat,
How we dressed,
How we walked,
We never bothered.
It was just our friends,
Our family
And us.

Entered our tween,
Something about us
Began to change
Within.
The first signs
Of adulthood,
Or so I think,
Began to shift

Our focus
Towards our looks.

A rush of emotions
We started to feel.
The hormones
Became active as a teen.
We became conscious
Of our body,
Our looks,
How we dressed.
We became obsessed.

The mirror became
Our favourite friend.
All the time
Looking
This way
And that way,
Not satisfied
With every change
That we made.

Lost focus
Of what is important
And dwelt
On the trivial,
Not realizing
That looks are
A fading phenomenon.
As we age,
We will lose it all.

What we were called
Or nicknamed
Bothered us
To the point
Of hurt.
Unable to reconcile
With how the world
Looked at us
With scorn.

Is there
Anybody there?
We shout
For rescue,
For help.
Does anybody understand
What we are going through?
Help us! Help us!
If you can.

Happy-to-help group: Building a healthy self-image through volunteering

Changing a Child's Perception

'When you change the way you look at things, the things you look at change.'

—Wayne Dyer

Not all are blessed with the right environment in their growing up years. Intentionally or unintentionally, comparisons are made between siblings, cousins, classmates or neighbourhood children without realizing the repercussions it can have on the child's psychology. Some are teased, some others body shamed, some for their stammer and stutter and some for being poor in studies. Some children retaliate, whereas others suffer silently. Elders' remarks can damage a child's life.

A teacher's greatness is in bringing to the surface what is within a child.

Some go on to become highly intelligent professionals but lack good self-esteem. They feel ashamed of themselves, their looks, their capabilities or their status. Whatever the reason may be, low self-esteem leads to difficulties in relationships and problems in school and at the workplace.

Children are not at peace with themselves. They are disturbed as they suffer from an inferiority complex.

They believe what the world says about them, look down on themselves, speak negatively, judge themselves and talk as if they are worthless. They try to fit into the world's definition of who they are. They become critical of themselves and endorse others' opinions of them, thereby overlooking their positive qualities.

The world's voice is too loud in their head. They develop the 'poor me' syndrome, which can even lead to depression, violent behaviour, suicidal tendencies, etc.

'How the world sees you makes a small difference. How you see yourself makes all the difference.'

—mahātria Rā

As a child, I had poor self-esteem. It took me many years to come out of it. It began with small victories I achieved in competitions when I was in school and when I started performing well in academics in school and college. I began to look up to myself. Your experiences help you understand people better. So, at NSN, we don't brand or label students. A child's wrong action is condemned but not the child. Even if any teacher resorts to such an action, the parents give us feedback because they understand that this is not NSN's culture.

'Believe in your infinite potential. Your only limitations are those you set upon yourself.'

—Roy T. Bennett

Each child has innate potential. Every teacher can be asked to identify the unique capabilities of their students. They can have a chart in class with the following heading: what next? It can have various columns like Word Smart, Number Smart, Picture Smart, Body Smart, Music Smart, People Smart, Dance Smart, Self-smart, etc. Have a list of student names on one side. You can design it according to your requirements. You can involve the students in this exercise, and they will be excited. They will be motivated to place a star under each column, that is, become smart in many ways. Teachers can also help students experience small victories that will boost their morale.

A child's socio-emotional well-being has to be nurtured with care. It helps with self-regulation and prevents negative behaviour. It is required to sustain meaningful relationships with adults and their peer groups. We can involve students in group activities and collaboration. We conduct brainstorming sessions every term wherein students come up with a solution for an existing problem. Students volunteer for school events. This makes them feel responsible and important. They learn to interact with a diverse group. The *Clean My School* campaign is done house-wise every month. The *Happy to Help* group ushers in kindergarten students every morning. Students are placed in different groups for all these activities. They are given equal opportunities and made to feel important. Mass counselling is also conducted. Every student meets the student counsellor one-on-one. Students can speak to the counsellor about how they feel and seek solutions.

Parents play a pivotal role in building a child's self-esteem. Hence, the school organizes sessions for the parents with the student counsellor to understand their children better.

Numerous historical figures, achievers and celebrities who had low self-esteem have become world-renowned personalities. We can talk to the students about them and, if need be, ask them to do role play to overcome the stumbling blocks in their lives. No matter what the world communicates to them, what they communicate to themselves makes all the difference. If they dismiss themselves, they become their own biggest enemy. Teaching them self-love will be the biggest turning point. The definition they use for themselves should change in their favour. The noise of others' opinions should not drown out their own inner voice. Let's change the child's perception of themself. They will begin to look up to themselves. All they need is motivation and the right approach from parents and teachers, who should be empowered by the school. Many educational institutions are doing this. That is why we call ourselves nation-builders!

I am Unique

A happy child is born
To doting parents
Who indulge and pamper
The apple of their eyes.
The love lasts
Till the first word
Of shame is uttered.

The child goes
Into a cocoon,
Unable to face the world,
Ashamed and conscious
Of being a lesser being,
Or so he thinks to be,
In the eyes of the world

The happy world
That was,
Ceases to exist.
A worse curse than this
Can never be
For the child
Who suffers silently.

A teacher
Affects eternity.
She can be
The guardian angel

To restore
The child's faith
In humanity.

Build his confidence,
Teach him to love himself,
Believe
That he can.
He is worth
Much more
Than he thinks.

Compare not
The capabilities,
Nor judge nor label.
Each child
Is God's gift.
Each child is UNIQUE!

Playing games is one of the ways to keep oneself fit

Fitness and Beyond

'Exercise not only changes your body; it changes your mind, your attitude and your mood.'

—Anonymous

For the last 20 years, I have been seeing a surge in the number of fitness studios in the city. With the advent of social media, one can access them from home. Online classes have become very common. Nevertheless, I also see many youngsters suffering from health issues, which could be due to work-related stress and an occupational hazard. In some cases, they burn out.

I realized the importance of fitness quite late in life, but once I did, I started paying attention to it and never compromised on it. I have been exercising for the last 20 years. I don't miss an opportunity to educate people on the importance of exercising regularly as I have personally experienced its benefits. In fact, we exercise as a family. I only share with people what I practice and avoid preaching. I always tell people that a healthy body is the best gift they can give themselves. Everything else in life is transient.

At the end of the year, our school receives resignation letters from teachers who have given up on their bodies. They confess that they are suffering from some health issues. I feel a sense of defeat when I see such letters because NSN pays so much attention to health and fitness. Most of us are women. By design, women often take care of the family to the detriment of their own health, not realizing that they can continue to take care of their loved ones only if they stay healthy.

As NSN focuses on the well-being of teachers, both physical as well as mental health, and addresses the same through sessions with the staff nurse and student counsellor, it has helped them discover if they have blood pressure issues and whether they are overweight and also if they need to work on their mental health. Quite a few started taking medication for blood pressure only after they started checking it every week. This became a blessing. Otherwise, it would have been fatal. The management also organized a complete blood test for the staff and arranged for doctors so that they could have a one-on-one review.

My daily routine of meditation and exercise gives me energy and vitality at the age of sixty-one. I feel energized throughout the day. Food also plays a vital role. I start with a salad and then protein, followed by fat and carbs. This order prevents sugar spikes. Many have told me that they don't have time to exercise, but I tell them to wake up a little early and create time for exercise. If we don't realize its importance now, we will have to regret it for the rest of our lives. Health truly is wealth. We educationists have more than enough challenges in our profession. Only a few things fall into our area of influence, and our health and fitness are some of them. When I give excuses to the world, I am actually giving excuses to myself without realizing it.

I was always fond of sleep, but to fit meditation into my morning routine, I wake up at 4.30 am. This gives me time to meditate for an hour. Educationists handle the emotions of the students, staff and parents. We need to work on our emotional equanimity first so as not to be disturbed by brickbats or get carried away by bouquets. We should be able to handle the highs and lows with maturity. Fitness should be an integral part of our daily life, as we always aspire to lead by example. Our fitness levels should motivate our staff. 'A sound mind in a sound body' after all.

Teachers have to stand for long hours, which takes a toll on their bodies if they don't exercise. We have to counter our daily activities with some form of exercise. Teachers invariably suffer from neck, back and knee pain. Correcting notebooks, standing for long hours, etc., makes them prone to these aches and pains.

We ask the student counsellor to address them on health, fitness and taking care of their body. We also invite guest speakers for an interactive session. One of our old students spoke to the women about polycystic ovary syndrome (PCOS). I am eager to know how else we can make them aware of the importance of taking care of their body.

I realize that it has to start very early in life. Hence, we have the Physical Literacy Programme for primary students. Fitness is for all, not just for those who are into sports. We also have a healthy snack timetable for students. Many parents have told me about its impact on children, as they counsel their parents to eat healthy food too.

Keep moving your body. Movement is key. The best gift we can give ourselves is a fit and healthy body. Are you there with me?

'Let's build wellness rather than treat diseases.'

—Bruce Daggy

Staying Fit

We are blessed
With a beautiful body,
Perfect in its function.
All it asks for
Is your kind attention.

An hour a day
Is all it needs
To feel
Robust,
Healthy and fit.

So much time
We give
To everything else,
But scant regard
For the most precious.

Love it to the core,
But do not pamper.
Move your body.
Twist and turn
Now and then.

Stretch it,
Bend it,
Load it
Every day
Without a miss.

Be sincere
To your body
To live
A healthy, happy
And a pain-free life.
Health is truly our wealth.

Expressing gratitude by honouring the support staff

Bouquet of Thanks

The school auditorium wore a festive look, and the student volunteers were busy arranging cards and gifts on the well-decorated table. The other students had already assembled there. The school assembly was conducted, and soon after, the function began. The school's support staff, including security personnel, janitors, housekeepers, drivers and conductors, were seated in the first few rows of the auditorium.

The announcement was in the regional language. Each person's name was called out and their work was described, and a long thank you was conveyed. Thereafter, the school band played high-pitched music befitting an Oscar awardee, and every staff member was escorted to the stage by two students. A Thank You card was handed over to the person, and a gift was presented. In this way, each staff member was honoured. Finally, a few of them came over to the mic and conveyed their joy at being recognized for their work. This is one day all the support staff look forward to.

A school has to go beyond textbooks, academics and the classroom to provide holistic education to the students. Learning happens everywhere and all the time as long as you keep the student within you alive. Students at NSN are blessed with many learning experiences and life-transforming opportunities. They are sensitized to the feelings of even the support staff in school. They will carry these experiences with them for the rest of their lives.

The security guard at the gate stands there throughout the day. It is a thankless job. If we can wish them with a smile while entering the school in the morning and thank them while leaving in the evening, they will experience immense joy. Students are told to do this. A heart filled with gratitude magnetizes abundance. All support staff are referred to as uncle and aunty by the students. They should learn to respect everyone from their formative years. They should not develop an attitude based on a person's social standing. Respect is beyond all that.

Children learn more from what they see than from what they hear. They learn much more from our actions. Even at home, when we treat domestic help with dignity, children learn to respect them. Our behaviour influences them. In their growing up years, if they are taught not to discriminate, they will treat everyone equally and with respect. Moreover, gratitude is the mother of all virtues. We need to be thankful for all the blessings in our lives. Right from the air we breathe to the bounties of life we enjoy, we need to be grateful. We need to be grateful to all the people in our lives.

Most of our miseries in life are because we forget to be grateful. You get what you celebrate. We need to bring an attitudinal shift in our thought process. Just take a moment out of your daily life to offer your gratitude to one and all. The Bouquet of Thanks is a day of celebration for everyone in the school. It reiterates that everyone is special. It takes a very small gesture to make people happy. Can we celebrate more such occasions where we make people feel special? It will definitely fill our hearts with overwhelming love for the people in our life.

'Living in a state of gratitude is our gateway to grace.'

—Arianna Huffington

Students being awarded for punctuality: Arriving on time is the first step towards a productive day

On-time All the Time

'Punctuality is not about being on time, it's basically about respecting your own commitments.'

—A.P.J. Abdul Kalam

The tiny tots in kindergarten were lined up to receive the On Time All The Time Award for their class. This award is given only when all students of a class are punctual to school every day for a month. Imagine a two-and-a-half-year-old or five-year-old coming to school on time every day! That is the culture we are promoting at NSN.

A punctuality certificate is given every month to all students who are punctual every day. It is our way of promoting punctuality and appreciating their commitment. What a world we can build if we train children to be responsible and committed individuals who are accountable for their actions! The vision of NSN is *'To take education beyond the classroom and contribute to a better world'*.

Who would be interested in working on a child's values and character other than the parents? This school is strongly focused on academics as well as students' personalities. If we are tough on them, life will be easy for them. Throughout their school life, if they put in the effort to be punctual, it will benefit them in many other areas of life.

Nothing will be a challenge for them. They will be more than willing to go the extra mile in their workplace too. They will develop resilience and become tough and disciplined. These qualities are conspicuous due to their absence in the world today.

People tend to give up easily in life. Any student who has passed through the doors of this august institution should be ready to conquer life! This is why the school insists on punctuality.

Was it easy to implement? Not at all. On one cloudy day, a few students came late. The parents who respected the school rules did not wait to argue but went away with their wards. A few of them insisted that their wards be allowed to attend class. They barged in like a mob and started yelling at the staff and speaking disrespectfully to the vice-principals in front of their wards, not realizing that they were setting a bad example for their children.

The otherwise serene school environment lost its sanctity due to the uncouth behaviour of these people. They lost their sense of decorum, hurled abuses at the school management and behaved in an uncivilized manner. The mother of one of the students instigated some of the others and convinced them to join her in a protest. She called the media (which is always looking for sensationalism), the police (who came with 10 others) and a politician. I calmly handled all of them, who were behaving unreasonably.

They persisted with me for over two hours, threatening and pressurizing me. Some parents barged into my room to take a video. It was later posted on social media and went viral. The public made very nasty remarks about the school. The media carried a news story about the school's unjustified action against the students. All this because the school insisted on punctuality! My heart beats for NSNites. Hence, I did not react.

'The world paves way for a resolute soul.'

—mahātria Rā

I had to pay a heavy price for trying to empower the students, but I convinced myself by saying that this is a world that assassinated Gandhi and crucified Christ for doing good. I knew that this too would pass. To stand by your principles in a world that does not agree with you needs a lot of courage. My deep faith and spiritual connection have always helped me be emotionally balanced in these situations. Nevertheless, amidst all this drama, the students regretted their parents' behaviour. They later shared this with the principal.

At times, society is against you. It is challenging to transform the mindset of the parents of 6,000 students, but we need to persist. When we reach critical mass, transformation occurs. NSN is only training students to stop giving excuses in life. Insisting on punctuality has a deeper meaning and purpose: to build a powerful subconscious mind. Excellence is zero defect.

If coming to school on time is such a challenge, how can we prepare children for greater obstacles in life? They will crumble in the face of difficulty. Instead of arguing against their growth, we need to encourage them to develop good habits. Our mind controls our actions. Taking control of our own minds is the biggest challenge we face. Programming the subconscious mind should be an important part of education. It should not be just about cramming for exams and securing good marks. Education should prepare students for life.

If you have not received a punctuality certificate yet, here is a plan for you. Prepare everything you require for the next day. Your books should be kept as per the timetable; your uniform should be ironed, and your shoes should be polished and kept along with your socks. Have a fixed time to wake up every morning. Get ready to go to school, and aim to reach 15 minutes before the bell so that you are on time. When you honour your commitment every day, you start believing in yourself. Eventually, the world will believe in you. This is how the 'I can' belief is built and the unfolding of a legend begins!

On-time, Every Time

Am I the master or a slave
To my habits?
We are what we repeatedly do,
Good or bad,
Right or wrong.
This is how habits form.

Where
Do I wish to reach?
What
Is the gap?
How
Do I bridge it?

On time, every time
Is a challenge,
But if you have the will
To achieve it,
You undoubtedly will
Conquer it.

Time is
A great resource,
Far too precious.
We realize it's worth
Only when
It leaves us.

NSN inculcates
A value for time.
It trains the mind
To embrace the right
And drop
That which is wrong.

Pain and pleasure,
The two
Dominant emotions
Control our life.
Only with discipline
We can make the right choice.

Strive to do what is right,
And feel liberated like the kite.
Easy and laid back
Never be.
Life is tough,
Just get ready.

Remember...
The power of the man
Lies in the
Power of his habits.
Never remain a slave
But a master of your life.

Social contribution: Creating responsible citizens

Responsible Citizenship

'Every good citizen adds to the strength of a nation.'

—Gordon B. Hinckley

Some incidents are forgotten, some leave a lasting impression on your mind, but some create a churning within you. I vividly recollect the scene I witnessed at a wedding reception. The guests were talking animatedly while eating at different counters on the lawn. They thoroughly enjoyed the food and ate without any restrictions. However, what irked me was the paper plates, tissues, fruit salad and chaat items lying on the floor of the lawn. It was very hard for me to believe that adults lacked grace and basic civic sense, the markings of a responsible citizen. In fact, I had half a mind to ask them all to pick it up and dispose of it in the trash bin. How could they do this in a public place? What were they teaching the little ones? That it is alright to litter, to throw food on the floor? To me, it was irresponsible behaviour. I just couldn't accept it.

I realized that reliving these scenes would only increase my anger. I thought it was better to work on my area of influence: the students in my school. Around that time, in 2014, our prime minister announced the Swachh Bharat Abhiyan to create a clean India. The school decided to use this opportunity to inculcate the habit of keeping one's surroundings clean in a novel way. We brainstormed on how to go about it. A plan was made that every Friday evening, the students and mentors of one of the four houses would clean the entire campus. Students were instructed to wear gloves and masks. Broomsticks and sticks for removing cobwebs were purchased. Areas were allotted for each group. The teachers were given a list of students for whom they were responsible and were asked to take attendance before and after the cleaning. It was named the 'Clean My School Campaign'.

It has been almost a decade since we started this wonderful practice. Cleaning the school every Friday has become a ritual. Students did it willingly. An Eco-friendly Class award was also instituted. Every class that is litter-free throughout the month is given this award during the morning assembly.

'Discover the joy of giving and you will discover the reason for living.'

—Mark Victor Hansen

To make them selfless individuals and to empower them to look beyond themselves, the school gets the students to collect funds from their family, friends and neighbours. Even staff members contribute to the fund. We have been doing this for over 25 years now. Students are told to talk to people about the less fortunate in society who need our help and the various social causes taken up by the school and seek their help. Little drops of water make a mighty ocean. So we collectively contribute towards a noble cause. We have built around 100 toilets for the underprivileged under the Prime Minister's Swachh Bharat Project on behalf of the local body. We have also contributed lakhs towards the Chief Minister's Relief Fund and many other projects, most of them for children, destitute women, healthcare, etc. Sharing and caring are an important part of the school curriculum.

The quickest and most effective way to transform adults is to convey the message through children. So we put up street plays on World Alcoholism Day, World Mental Health Day, avoiding plastic to save the environment, etc. They are performed in the regional language as it has a wider reach. This is done to instil social responsibility in students. They do it with considerable enthusiasm. Parents support us unconditionally in these matters. We took around nine days to complete the *Go Green* project. Students enthusiastically walked around the streets. The local body supported us by digging the pits. Certificates were given to all participants. Today, those saplings have grown into huge trees. This is a legacy we will leave behind.

Visits to old age homes and homes for abandoned children, spending a day with them, serving them and carrying eatables for them are regular features. The students are taken for temple cleaning, wall painting, forest cleaning, etc., as part of their Scouts and Guides and the Junior Red Cross activities. After leaving the school, some students continue contributing to a social cause. Some of them came together and started an educational trust that sponsors the education of children from underprivileged families; some of them have founded NGOs, and the list goes on.

Water and electricity are very precious resources that should not be wasted. The school has installed solar power panels to reduce the cost of our power consumption. We make students conscious about saving energy. Once a month, we ask them to observe Earth Hour by switching off the lights and fans at home for an hour. This makes them conscious about the depletion of these resources. Any resource can be used but not wasted.

As much as we focus on academics, we also focus on giving the students horizontal exposure. A school is not only a temple of learning but also a temple of transformation. We should give children all the right experiences when they are growing up. Immersing children in such activities keeps them engaged and makes them contributing citizens. Giving is an attitude. Nation-building is a huge responsibility that is shared by parents and teachers. What kind of individual we send into society makes all the difference. Right parenting and good schooling can help uplift a nation.

'If not us, who? If not now, then when?'

—John Lewis

Make Your Life Count

Learning, earning and returning
Are not different phases
But concurrent.
Some earn
While they learn.
But how many return?

Giving is an attitude,
So is sharing and caring.
Attitudes must be shaped
When you are young.
Learn to look beyond
Me, mine and myself.

The world needs you.
Lend your hand.
Choose to be selfless
And never heartless.
The force above
Will bless you with abundance.

Clean India, green India
Should be your goal.
Take every effort
To keep your country clean.
Swachh Bharat Abhiyan
Should be your dream.

Never miss to be of help
To others and not just yourself.
The joy of giving,
The joy of loving
Are experiences
That are priceless.

Be a responsible citizen
And a good Samaritan.
Strive to be a role model
And one above the crowd.
Put your hand up,
And make your life count!

Guru Vandanam: Gratitude is the mother of all virtues

Attitude of Gratitude

'Education is the most powerful weapon which you can use to change the world.'

—Nelson Mandela

So many students have passed through the doors of this august institution. Very few come back to thank the teachers or the school for where they have reached in life. Once they become adolescents, their behaviour changes. Some of them even involve their ego with their parents. They talk to them with disrespect. Some parents have cried bitterly while sharing this with us. We teach our children so many things, but the most important value to be ingrained in them is gratitude. You may wonder why *mata*, *pita*, *guru* and *deivam* are the four creators of our life. They enjoy an exalted status in the universe. That's the design of life. We are nothing without them. The first three are equal to God. We need to correct our feelings towards them no matter how they are. How we relate to them decides our well-being. Our traditions and culture help us live a beautiful life. Mocking the creators of our lives or disregarding them only contributes to our misery. In fact, our hearts should beat in gratitude every moment of our lives.

To fill the students' hearts with gratitude for their teachers, the school observes Guruvandanam on Guru Poornima Day every year. Students from classes 1–12 participate in this ceremony. It is a very solemn occasion. Students assemble class-wise in the auditorium. The air is filled with the chanting of 'Gurur Brahma,

Gurur Vishnu...' A lamp is lit, and the school choir sings the *shloka* 'Deepam Jyoti Parabrahma'. This is followed by a soulful rendition of 'Maithreem Bhajatha'. Then, a student speaks about the significance of Guruvandanam, after which students come to offer their respect to their teachers by offering flowers at their feet and prostrating. Finally, the choir sings 'Asathoma Sath Gamaya'. The teachers come together and bless the students by showering rice grains on them while they stand in the auditorium with their heads bowed down in reverence. This is the culmination of the sacred ceremony. Participating in it creates an inexplicably overwhelming feeling.

Such experiences will certainly transform the students' minds over the years. Action-feeling is a cycle. The way you act causes certain feelings in you and the way you feel propels certain actions in you. They will learn to connect with their teachers, and the teachers will build good relationships with their students. In many families, the bond between parents and children is missing. Parents are unable to accept the ways of the younger generation, not realizing that we need to adapt to changing times without compromising on values. Children also take their parents for granted. They don't realize their contributions. Children have learnt to value things and use people instead of using things and valuing people.

> 'Gratitude unlocks the fullness of life. It turns what we have into enough, and more.'
>
> —Melody Beattie

Children's Day is celebrated as Thanksgiving Day in our school. On this day, children convey their love and gratitude to their parents. On the preceding day, they are asked to bring all the materials required to prepare a beautiful card for their parents. They are made to realize their parents' significant role in their lives. This teaches them to be grateful to their parents. On Children's Day, they give the card to their parents before coming to school. There have been instances of parents reading the card and becoming overwhelmed. Parents and children hug each other and cry out of joy. These are some beautiful memories I cherish as an educationist. My role enables me to act as a catalyst in bringing a paradigm shift in the minds of students, thereby creating a beautiful world.

> *'Be thankful for what you have; you'll end up having more. If you concentrate on what you don't have, you will never, ever have enough.'*
>
> —Oprah Winfrey

The day at school begins with students invoking the blessings of the Almighty. They again thank God for the food they are blessed with before lunch, and at the end of the day, they reiterate their gratitude before leaving. Even a morsel of food we eat is God's blessing. We should be grateful for the blessings in our lives. An awareness is created in children to be grateful for every moment of their lives. Many less fortunate and underprivileged people in the world are deprived of several things. Should we not acknowledge what we are blessed with? Only then will life present us with more instances to be grateful. If I keep complaining, only such instances will repeat in my life. The school handbook has a few pages for a gratitude journal in which children can write daily about what they are grateful for. Children are also encouraged to have a gratitude jar at home. All family members can fill it up with their gratitude chits. When we have the power to transform the world, we should not miss out on this golden opportunity.

Love does not have just one meaning. It defines the bond of so many relationships. To broaden their perspective of love, which is so integral to every relationship, Valentine's Day is celebrated as the Joy of Loving. Students are asked to express their love and gratitude to someone, other than their parents, who has played a significant role in their life. Students make a card and give it to their uncles, aunts and grandparents, who they think have immensely influenced or inspired them. At times, the card is given to the auto/van driver who brings them to school. It is so touching to hear these stories and realize that we are able to build a new world by inculcating the right values in them. Schooling is not just about educating the minds of our youth; it is about educating their hearts too.

'Gratitude and disturbance cannot coexist. If you are disturbed, it only means you are not grateful in those moments.'

—mahātria Rā

A Grateful Heart

Gratitude is an attitude
None is born with.
It is inculcated
Over the years
And takes birth
In the deep recess of the heart.

When the heart
Is bereft of it,
Misery fills our life,
The mind is tossed,
The heart bleeds
And we cry in pain and agony.

One small quality
Missing in man
Unknown to him
Can take away his peace
And bear no fruit
For all his hard work.

Complaining is a habit
To be done away with.
It becomes a burden
And takes away the lustre
From our otherwise blessed life,
Which we need to cherish.

When the heart beats
In eternal gratitude,
Life blossoms
In joy and happiness.
The rhythm of life
Is restored in abundance.

Mindfully we shall live,
Remembering to thank
Every goodness
We are blessed with.
The Almighty shall be pleased
And bless us with most and more.

Spirituality in Education

'In everything, the higher and the deeper can be experienced.'

—mahātria Rā

The school's 40th Annual Day was a very special one because that was the first time my spiritual guru visited our school. Before leaving, we asked Him to write in the Visitors' Book, not realizing that He was not meant to be a mere visitor in my life but would permanently reside in me to rewrite my destiny. He wrote thus, 'An individual finds a Cause. The individual carries the Cause forward. A day comes when the Cause starts carrying the individual forward. I think something like that is happening to NSN. I am always with the Cause called NSN.' My ego was annihilated that day, and I realized that I was a mere instrument in His hands. I stopped taking credit for NSN's growth. 'Thy will be done' was an awakening! There was total surrender to God at that moment. I realized that I need God's grace to achieve my dreams.

From then on, I started seeing NSN differently. 'Lead me forward,' became my prayer. I touch the floor of the school every morning before stepping in and whisper a silent prayer, 'Thank you, God, for choosing me as Thy instrument and for making my life count. I am truly blessed!' My work became my prayer unto Him. I thought that if spirituality could bring a huge transformation in me, it could do wonders for the students, who were young and at an impressionable age. The real world is far from ideal with cut-throat competition, commerce without morality, perversion, crumbling values, pleasure without conscience, knowledge without character and wealth without work. Can't we bring all these within our circle of influence? If somebody can change society and make it a better place for people to live, only the parents of the future citizens of the country and educationists, the two great influencers of the world, can do so. Such is the power of education and educationists.

To make them spiritually aligned, we introduced some of our best practices, which will aid in their holistic growth and help them live a quality life, wherein they have better self-control, self-discipline and awareness about life's experiences. Spirituality does not mean sitting in meditation alone. Bringing in qualities of love, gratitude, happiness, selflessness, responsibility, accountability, etc., to their personality is also growing spiritually. It also helps achieve calmness and inner peace in a chaotic world and establish better relationships, improved health, a clear understanding of themselves and empathy in their hearts, eventually making them aware of their own actions and helping them live a more meaningful life.

The Willpower Drive helps them achieve a state of mind over body. It helps them to develop a powerful mind, which helps them to make the right choices, by using their intellect, and not get carried away by what gives them pleasure. Outside every classroom, we have the wisdom of infinitheism that the students see every day. We believe in the power of subliminal learning as it has a great impact on their adult life. So, the right exposure will lead them to the right actions.

Thus, experiences are created to teach them to share and care for fellow human beings, spread awareness regarding the ill effects of wrong habits, protect the environment, keep the environment clean, develop integrity, happily help others, find good in others, build self-confidence, use self-affirmations to make their life count, not indulge in violence, to dream big and live a glorious life, which helps them grow in their own eyes.

Students may not understand, but the school has to immerse them in these experiences. After 15 years of school education that deepens their awareness and reiterates positive thinking, students are bound to emerge as world-class citizens who will bring glory to the country and make this world a better place for all. That would be our best contribution to the world!

Spiritual Alignment

Knowledge is power.
It is a passport
To my future.
It qualifies me
For the positions I hold
And provides me with a living.

Gratitude is a virtue.
It fills my heart with thankfulness,
Helps me count
My blessings and beyond,
Brings in contentment
And happiness in life.

Love all, love all the time.
It is a giving emotion.
Don't wait to receive.
Starvation for love
Ceases only by loving
The world.

What you think,
So you become.
Ask not
Will I be caught or not?
Always ask
Am I right or not?

The power of the man
Is the power of his mind.
The right attitude,
Right direction
Is what we need
In life.

Life does not care
Who you are.
Are you aligned
To the truth
Of life?
Alignment is key.

To live a balanced life
Of this and that,
Materialistic success
Integrated with spiritual rootedness
Is the preparation for life.
NSN is a game-changer!

Building powerful minds through meditation

One Best Practice of NSN

'To take education beyond the classroom and to contribute to a better world.'

When this is NSN's vision, achieving such a lofty ideal is not an easy task. Yet, a vision is not for achieving but journeying towards. Hence, we have to constantly keep reinventing ourselves. What works today may not work tomorrow. To sustain itself and keep progressing is definitely challenging for a 56-year-old institution. Generations have passed out of this august institution, and it now has to cater to the present generation—Gen Z.

NSN always assumes responsibility for grooming a child's personality. Academics and skill development are not our only focus; we prepare them for life after school. Consequently, attitudes, values and discipline are given considerable importance. Ideally, the school's efforts should be complemented at home by parents so that the child gets the best of both worlds. Getting the man right to get the world right is an arduous task. All the school's activities are designed in this direction, with the child as the nucleus.

One of NSN's best practices, if I may say so, is making students sit in non-doing first thing in the morning. They sit in silence for 11 minutes. It will help them to focus, to elevate their energy levels and bring clarity to their thinking. We firmly believe that the mind of the person is the person. It is crucial to develop a powerful mind so that dropping a bad habit or picking up a good habit is a decision without struggle.

The struggle in today's world is to uphold commitments. Moreover, instead of doing what is right, people choose to do what is easy and convenient. Social media are highly influential. People are getting carried away by everything they see and hear. Instead of improving their lives, they are more interested in prying into others' lives. Values and discipline are on the decline. Instant gratification has become normalized. The question is no longer of right or wrong but if they will be caught or not. Hence, there is a dire need for students to connect with themselves, as there is a lot of chaos in their minds. The only way to calm them down and create heightened awareness is through meditation. This alone will help their higher qualities to prevail over their lower qualities.

> 'Science:
> Through education
> Fill your mind.
> Spirituality:
> Through meditation
> Empty your mind.'
>
> —mahātria Rā

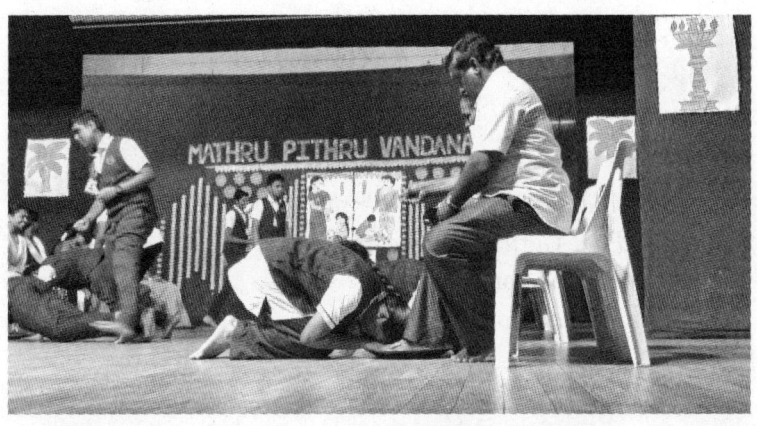

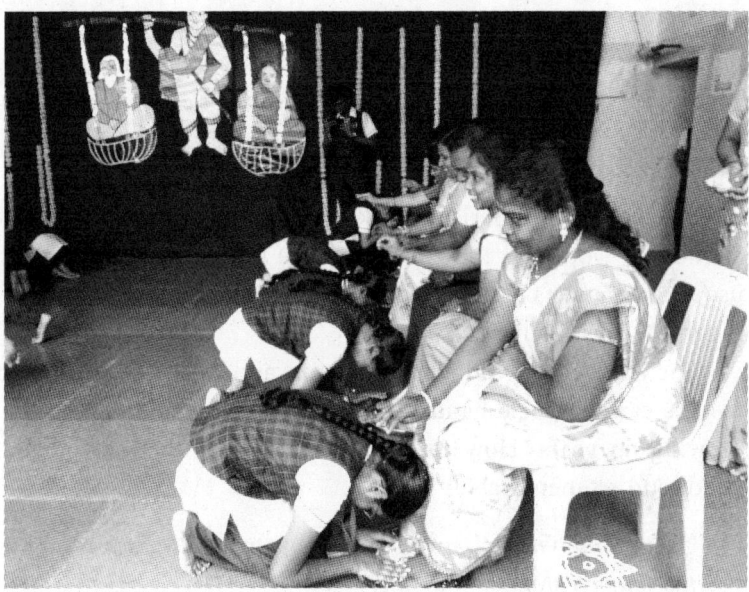

Matru–Pitru Vandanam: Bowing in reverence to the creators of our life

Mata, Pita, Guru, Deivam

'Begin and end your day with salutations to
Mata, Pita, Guru, Deivam.
Simply express your gratitude
To the four creators of your life.'

—mahātria Rā

When I reminisce about my childhood, my face lights up and my lips part into a smile. My heart does not beat 'lub–dub, lub–dub'; instead, it beats, 'Thank you. Thank you.' My mother raised three daughters as a single parent with no one to help her. Yet, she gave us a beautiful childhood that we will always cherish. The kind of comfort we enjoyed, the clothes we wore and the chocolates she bought us never made us feel our father's absence even once. As an adult, I realize how tough life was for her.

She was a young widow at thirty-one and had three daughters to take care of single-handedly. I have no complaints about my growing-up years. How thankful I am to her for making my childhood so memorable!

'Mata, Pita, Guru, Deivam are all one without a second—
the four creators of your life.'

—mahātria Rā

Though the three are embodied, they enjoy a divine status. Understanding that our parents are the greatest blessing in our lives and knowing how important it is for us to remain ever grateful to them, I thought I should instil this quality in our students. Many do not even acknowledge their parents' role in their lives. Sometimes, it is their ignorance. They take their parents for granted. Children have to be told and be made aware. It will be great if the school can do this.

When our heart is filled with gratitude, more instances will occur in our lives to be grateful. The more we complain, the more that such instances will occur in our lives. This is the basic premise upon which the universe works. I have experienced both, so I can validate it. Mata, pita and guru are equal to God. They enjoy an exalted status in the universe. We need to correct our feelings towards them, regardless of how they are towards us.

I have a positive mental icon for all the people who matter to me. It is good for me to have the right thoughts and feelings about them. Even those who have hurt me, betrayed me or not treated me well, I have learnt from them how not to be, and I am thankful to them for teaching me this vital lesson. Positive feelings towards people make you feel good and energize you. Negative feelings drain you of energy.

Gratitude is an important part of NSN's curriculum. The school handbook has a page for a gratitude journal. Students also post a sticky note in the 'Tree of Joy', which provides a space for expression. With the advent of social media, I have noticed a big shift in the behaviour of many parents. Consequently, children find it very difficult to look up to them. We decided to help children develop great regard for their parents by giving them the right perspective and helping them celebrate their parents.

'As we think, so we become.' Children's thought process is directed through activities that will usher in the inner flowering of their personality.

It is said that if we fail to see divinity in the three creators of our lives, we will be unable to experience divinity in the formless presence: Deivam. Empowering children to see everything and everyone from the right perspective is a huge responsibility for educationists.

> 'It is sathyam that so much about your life will turn right by just getting your feelings towards Mata, Pita, Guru and Deivam right.
> It is the law.
> It is the truth.'
>
> —mahātria Rā

The Creators of My Life

Happily, I emerged
From your womb.
You nurtured me
With love and care.
I grew up as your child,
Feeling secure
In your lap.

You were my playmate
And then my confidante.
You alone understood me.
You were my strength.
Your face never revealed
Even if you were in pain.
Years went by,
And you became
My child, my mom.

From my childhood,
You were my toy.
The elephant rides
Are vivid still.
You gave me power
And pushed me
To be strong and confident.

I was reluctant
To cry in your presence

As I wanted you
To be ever
Proud of me.
You had more ambitions
for me than I had.
A great life
You provided me, my dad.

School was home
As you were there
Every morn
With a smile
To receive me
And take me
Along with you.

Oh, my Guardian Angel!
How much I cherish
The days I spent
Learning and unlearning.
You kept repeating
The dos and don'ts in life
Till I mastered them.
You created me
And shaped my future, my teacher!

I always saw
Only the form,
Far away
Enshrined and untouched.
Sang Thy praises,
Chanted Thy name
In a thousand ways.

Spiritual evolution in life
Helped me to see Thee
Within me.
I realized that
You are nearer than the nearest.
You are me,
And I am You.
We are in unison
As I was, in my mother's womb!

Dear Educators,

Thank you so much for picking up *Beyond the Bell*. I am sure your passion for providing better education has created the curiosity in you to go through this book. I am excited to share our best practices and insights with you, and I am sure this book will serve as a valuable resource in your own educational journey.

As educators ourselves, we understand the challenges and opportunities that come with implementing new ideas. Hence, I want to assure you that our support doesn't end with the purchase of this book.

Team NSN is committed to helping you implement the best practices outlined in this book. I invite you to reach out to us for guidance, support and connection. As educators, let us unite to create a nurturing environment that instils values, discipline and responsibility in our students, empowering them to become conscientious citizens who contribute positively to society.

I would be happy to hand-hold you through the process and answer any questions you may have, to help you on your way. You can contact me at nsncorrespondent@gmail.com or 9363876455. I look forward to connecting with you and supporting you on your journey to excellence in education.

Thank you once again for your interest in the book. I am honoured to be a part of your educational journey.

Best regards,
Chitra Prasad